A Collection of 12 Life-Changing Short Stories

Volume 1

J Alexander

This book may not be reproduced, transmitted or stored in whole or in part by any means including graphic, electronic or mechanical without the express written consent of the publisher except in the case of brief quotations embodied in critical articles and reviews.

For more information about the authors or other publications
Email: tclc@rogers.com
Website: sosop.ca

Formatted and produced for printing by

Visit **www.outinfront.ca** or
email **susanlamb12@rogers.com**for more info

First Edition
Published in Canada

Dedication

*I dedicate this short story collection
to persecuted Christians
around the world, and I pledge to use the
money raised from not only this project,
but all monies, from my many
fundraising programs to spread the
Gospel of Jesus Christ
to all mankind.*

Contents

	Your Attention Please	i
	Introduction	iii
1	Honor they Father and Mother	1
2	Do Unto Others	7
3	Dust on the Bible	15
4	Does Two Wrongs Ever Make A Right	25
5	Angels Among Us	39
6	Sin City	45
7	The Anniversary	69
8	Paid In Full	77
9	Anger Destroys Everything	83
10	Enter Shakespeare	103
11	The Long Black Train	137
12	Robbed Blind	161
	Notes and Thoughts	
	About the Author	
	More Great Stuff To Check Out	
	Contact and Ordering	

Your Attention Please:

I know for a fact that you have had many dreams, and probably not many have come true. Well, I'm no different than you. I have an unfailing hope in my God that whatever I do in the name of Jesus, He will give me the strength to be the person He wants me to be, so I can do the things that will glorify His Holy name.

Every Christian has an obligation to advance God's Kingdom. "You can't do everything, but you can do something, you can't help everyone, but you can help someone."

I'm asking you today to join my team, and help me to bring my dreams to life. Projects like, SOSCC.ca, SOSOP.ca, "The Christian Life Collection," Shipwreck and a road called Grief, "The Passport Series," turning this collection of 12 short stories into Plays, short films, and maybe a TV series.

When you check out these opportunities and make a commitment to get involved, you will begin to see how they can not only help you realize your dreams, but can change the lives of every person in your life.

With Respect,

The Author
J Alexander

Please contact me today at:

Office: 1-905-238-3547
1-416-500-8207

Email: soscc@rogers.com
sosop@rogers.com

Websites: SOSCC.ca
SOSOP.ca

Introduction

This collection of short stories (except for "Robbed Blind" story number 12) were taken from my novel "Shipwreck and a road called Grief by J Alexander".

It says in the Bible, that even Jesus asked God to take away his cup of suffering. So could anyone of us mere mortals claim to be greater than He? I think not.

The inspiration for these short stories came from John Bunyan's "Pilgrim's Progress" a timeless masterpiece and also his life's story. Even Mr. Bunyan's last words have endured for over four-hundred years, "Weep not for me, but for your selves. I go to the Father of our Lord Jesus Christ, who will through the mediation of His blessed Son receive me though a sinner; there we shall meet to sing the new song and remain everlastingly happy, world without end."

If you want to move on with your life, just listen to what God has to say:

"I know your heart is hurting today. It hurts to think and breathe. It hurts to remember. It hurts to think about going forward. In these moments, I want to challenge you to stop, breathe, and think of me. I will give you hope for the future that at this moment you simply can't comprehend."

If only one suffering, grieving person (Soul) finds some comfort in just one story I will consider the entire project a success.

Story One

Honor they Father and Mother

"Honor thy father and mother - that your days may be long upon the land which the Lord your God is giving you."
(The Fifth Commandment)

As David read the sign "Come and ride on the Reflection and Guilt Train" it didn't exactly bestow confidence; as a matter of fact, it was a little intimidating. Mustering all his courage, he opened the little white gate and walked the twenty or so feet to the front steps. After a slight hesitation he started climbing, thinking to himself, "Oh well, I've come this far; I may as well see this through."

Standing at the front door, David wasn't worried that someone might hurt him physically; but what he did know was that a person's hurtful words could cut you right to the bone.

After taking a deep breath, he knocked three times and then waited. When he didn't hear any movement from inside the house, he thought, "Now what'll I do? Should I leave, wait or knock again?"

His question was answered by a voice from the other side of the door. "Who are you and what do you want?"

"Hello, my name is David and I was wondering if I could talk to you for a few moments?"

"What do you want to talk about?"

"I was told you could help me. I have a major 'Anger' problem."

The door opened just a little and an unshaven, and very worried looking man said, "Take a seat over there and I will be with you in a minute."

David had just settled into one of the patio chairs when a short little balding man came out of the house. Sitting down across from David he asked, "Can I get you anything?"

Without waiting for a reply, he stood up and put out his hand saying, "Hi, my name is Sammy. I guess I'll start by telling you my story and then you can tell me how I can help you."

Sammy shared his story! "Sad to say, I've lived in this small town all my life. My Mom died a few years ago and my Dad took it pretty hard. After a few years he seemed to be coming around and then one day I noticed he was acting very strange. I thought it was Alzheimer's taking over his mind."

As he spoke, he spread out a bunch of cards on the patio table. "Anyway, I had to work every day so Pop was alone most of the time. Although he never talked about what he did during the day, I could see that he was reverting back to his childhood.

Every day when I got home I'd find him sitting in the kitchen and he would be covered from head to toe in dirt.

I also noticed that he had cuts, blisters and calluses from his elbows to his fingertips."

"This went on for quite a while until one day, in the middle of the summer; I received a call from the fire department advising me that there was a fire that had started in the kitchen at my home. The worst part about it was that the front and back doors were wide open, but there was no one in the house. The smoke alarm went off and the fire department was called.

Dad showed up just after the firemen, admitting that he had put something on the stove but then got busy and forgot all about it."

"I arranged to have a meeting with the fire chief and my alarm company. They suggested I consider hiring someone to be with my dad all day or place him in a home."

"When I returned home from work that evening, my dad was nowhere to be found; I started walking up the street and in a few minutes I located him. He was carrying an old beat up vacuum cleaner.

He smiled when he saw me but I wasn't smiling. I was very angry that he was out in public dragging around garbage like a homeless person. I grabbed his arm and told him to throw that dirty old thing in the garbage. Hanging onto the vacuum cleaner like a spoiled child, he insisted, 'I'm going to fix it up as good as new'."

"My anger was getting the best of me as I dragged and pushed my once very proud father along the street to our home."

When we got into the hallway I let my father have it. 'You're embarrassing me, Dad! People are laughing at you; don't you care? If you don't stop what you're doing, I'm going to have to put you in a home where they know how to treat people like you, who have lost their mind'."

His story went on; "Dad was looking down at the floor and not paying any attention to me. This made me so angry that I knocked the vacuum out of his hand. As he stood there like a little child, I shouted at him, 'I'm tired of looking after you; why don't you do us both a favor and die'?"

"As Dad got down on one knee, and started picking up the pieces of the vacuum cleaner, he looked up at me and said, 'I'm sorry I disappointed you son'. That was the last thing I heard him say, as he grabbed his chest and fell quietly to the floor."

"I was so scared I didn't know what to do! I had never witnessed anyone having a heart attack so I just rolled him over and begged him to get up. As I knelt beside him I cried, 'Please don't die Dad; I didn't mean what I said.'

"After a few minutes, reality set in, and I rushed to the phone and called 911.

I knew in my heart that the call was not an emergency, because like my mom, my father was now in heaven and

I was left to spend the rest of my life all alone."

"There were about fifteen people that day at the cemetery as we laid my father to rest next to mom.

After the ceremony, I was surprised at all the wonderful things people were saying about my dad. That evening, I read the cards and realized that my father was not the mentally disturbed man I thought he was, on the contrary; he was loved by all who knew him.

He wasn't roaming the streets looking for garbage; he was repairing things and helping his neighbors with their everyday chores; people like old man Oliver with his garden or John O'Malley who was fixing up an old car for his son to drive. As a matter of fact, almost everyone who lived on Anger Street got help from my father at one time or another."

Unable to say anything to comfort Sammy, David stood up and started walking down the stairs. For some unknown reason he could clearly see the Bible showing the commandment of honoring your parents. It read: "that your days may be long upon the land which the Lord your God is giving you." If you continue to honor your parents through your lifetime, your children will see the example and hopefully get the message.

As a child my parents or anyone who came in contact with me always chalked my anger up to me being a spoiled brat. I will admit to being spoiled, but my anger even shocked me, when it got out of control."

David was in awe as he listened and mentally recorded the woman's story. She continued on, "My teachers, parents and even my few friends didn't mess with me and if they did, it was only once. To me, life was great but to everyone else around me, it was a living hell. Because I was so hard to get along with, I spent a lot of time alone, but when I did give an order or yelled, things got done and done my way. I enjoyed watching my two kids, Michael and Jennifer; literally jump when I shouted out an order.

Now my husband Anthony, he was a different story. He didn't talk much and that was okay, but he would make me furious when I would tell him to do something and he would smile at me and then just walk away. I've thrown a few objects his way in the past, but that didn't faze him at all. He would just smile and leave the room." |

"As for my home, I wanted the best of everything from furniture and paintings to a professionally landscaped and manicured property. To have the best, you have to hire the best and that is what I did. My dear sweet loving husband was very rich so money was never a problem."

Story Two

Do Unto Others

When wise people speak, they make knowledge attractive, but stupid people spout nonsense.
Proverbs 15:2

Looking at the house and the condition of the front yard, David was sure that this home at # 2 Anger Street didn't do much to promote the resale values of the homes in the neighborhood.

Walking up the unpainted steps to the front porch, he could see an elderly woman in a rocking chair, but as he got closer to her, he realized she just looked old and that she was probably only in her early fifties.

Without asking permission, David sat on a chair beside the woman. Not looking at him she said, "I know why you're here; you want to know if I have ever experienced Anger."

Through clenched rotten teeth, the woman remarked, "Young man, you're looking into the face of anger! I was an angry child, an angry teen and I continue being angry to this day. Some people sarcastically called me 'Little Miss Penelope,' but that never bothered me.

David looked a little confused because from where he was sitting, the place definitely did not fit her description of a dream home.

"I can see by the expression on your face that you're thinking this can't be the place I'm describing. Well you're right; I haven't always lived here. Come with me and I'll show you where I used to call home."

Following her to the end of the veranda, David looked in the direction of her outstretched hand. He had to catch his breath as he gazed upon a very large castle perched on top of a hill.

Smiling for the first time she turned to David; "That's where I was a 'Fairytale Queen' ruling over all my subjects. I know I would still be there if I had controlled my anger, but then my story would have a happy ending instead of…well, as you can see, things don't always turn out the way they're planned."

We sat down again and she continued telling her story. "I was in the habit of interviewing anyone who wanted to do work at the Castle. All individuals, companies and contractors would be interrogated by yours truly."

"One contractor, a little mouse of a man named Mr. Hornsby, had a great reputation in the horticulture industry. He owned a chain of flower shops that catered to the rich.

I was planning to use him for some small projects in the spring of the year and if he worked out okay I would use him for my big event in the summer. Well my events weren't really little tea parties; they were full blown galas. All the upper class would be there, so I wanted everything to be perfect. Nothing less would be acceptable.

After interviewing Mr. Hornsby and using him for two of my smaller venues, I signed a contract for his company to provide the floral arrangements for my big extravaganza."

"The day of the big summer event was hectic, to say the least. Everything was fine until I counted the rose arrangements on the tables. One of the vases had eleven roses instead of the twelve that was agreed upon. I was so angry and upset that I was seeing red and it wasn't the reflection from the roses!"

I couldn't control myself and I hollered out, 'Someone bring me Mr. Hornsby now!' I was getting more frustrated by the minute, as I stood there tapping my fingers on the table. I screamed again, 'Will someone get that little…on the phone before I explode?'

"One of the servants called out, 'I have his office on the phone and they say he's tending to a personal matter and can't be reached.'

"I want you to phone back and tell them that if he's not here within the hour, he will wish he had never gone into business! The more I looked at the vase with the missing rose, the madder I got. Guests were starting to arrive, but I was so embarrassed I couldn't get up to greet them. My husband Anthony did the best he could, but he was not used to being the host."

"Within a half hour most of the guests had arrived, some were seated and others were just standing around listening to the orchestra playing classical music. People could sense that the 'Queen Bee' was in one of her moods and it was just a matter of time before I exploded."

"The guests didn't have to wait long for the inevitable to happen. This was not the first time they had seen me in action, but what was about to unfold was even above and beyond anything they had ever seen. Everyone knew something was up when they saw a man coming down the stairs to the right of the orchestra and heard me holler out, 'Stop right there Mr. Hornsby, you need to account for your inferior service.'

"After pushing my chair back so hard that it crashed to the floor, I strutted right up to the microphone and pushed the band leader out of the way and then I proceeded to do the unthinkable… I summoned Mr. Hornsby to come to the queen.

The stunned audience gave a gasp of disbelief as they watched me slap the defenseless little man not once, but twice.

I then grabbed him with both hands and turned him toward my shocked guests and said, 'This pathetic excuse for a man will now explain to all of us why there are only eleven roses in this vase, when I specifically ordered twelve. After that he will explain why he has kept me waiting for two hours.'

"Red faced and barely able to speak, Mr. Hornsby addressed the crowd."

'First of all I want to apologize to Miss. Penelope, her family and to you, her special guests. I don't know how my employee could have miscounted the roses, but I take full responsibility for ruining this perfect day. The reason I couldn't get here sooner was because three hours ago, I was informed by the police that my wife Jan and our two kids were involved in a head on collision. The emergency room doctor said they have taken my wife and son into surgery and that my precious daughter Sarah was in a coma and she may not survive the night.'

"With tears running down his face and a lump in his throat, Mr. Hornsby said, 'I'm truly sorry for any inconvenience or embarrassment I may have caused any of you here today.'

"A silence fell over the crowd as they watched a broken and devastated man walk slowly up the stairs and then out of sight. Not a word was said as each guest rose to their feet and followed in Mr. Hornsby's footsteps."

"Looking for support from her family, Penelope held out her hand and said, 'I didn't know;' 'it's not my fault;'

"I just wanted everything to be perfect. Anthony, you understand don't you?"

"No, I certainly do not. As a matter of fact, I'm disgusted by your actions today and I want you to leave."

Holding his two devastated children he said, "Goodbye Penelope, I'll have my lawyer contact you tomorrow.

"Now you know the story Sir. I lost everything because of my lifetime of anger. I sit here most nights and look up at that mansion on the hill and curse the day I was born. I do feel a little bit better after sharing my story with you. You're a good listener, just like that fellow who was here a few weeks ago.

After hearing my story, he just shook his head and said, 'I'm sorry your life turned out this way,' and then he gave me his Bible. He told me, 'If you read the place I have marked and believe what it says, you will find some comfort in your sad and lonely life.'

Handing the Bible to David she said, "I wish I had my life to live over so I could do what the Bible says:" *Ephesians 4: 31, 32.*

Get rid of all bitterness, passion, and anger. No more shouting or insults, no more hateful feelings of any sort. Instead, be kind and tender-hearted to one another, and forgive one another, as God has forgiven you through Christ.

With tears building up inside of him, David said, "You can't go back and change the past, but you can alter your future. It's plain to see that God has forgiven you, but now it's up to you to forgive yourself. Only when you come to terms with your anger and accept your past will you be able to move on with your life."

The woman looked at David and replied, "I ask only one thing of you; please tell my story to others, and if my worthless life helps just one person, then my life will not have been lived in vain."

After looking back at the house one more time, then closing the gate, David noticed the envelope sitting on the "Little Golden Bench." But like "# 1 Anger Street," he didn't feel he needed encouraging words to help him go on, so he started walking toward his next assignment.

Story Three

Dust on the Bible

Hot tempers cause arguments, but patience brings peace
Proverbs 15: 18

When David finally made it back to "Anger Street," he was surprised to see an ambulance pulling out of house number three. This was to be his next stop, but he hesitated going in, knowing the people who lived there would probably not be receptive to a stranger dropping in to have a little chat.

What he did know, was that he needed to finish his assignment. His new burden "Anger" had given him strict instructions to follow and so far he was making good time, with only three more houses to visit.

David was talking to himself saying, "I'll just say hello to the home owner and tell them that I can come back at a more convenient time." He had his head down as he walked toward the house and didn't see the woman standing at the top of the front steps.

As she started walking down to meet him, she said in a low voice, "I'm Jan Bushnell, how may I help?"

Looking up, David smiled and answered, "I was wondering if we could arrange a meeting to talk about 'Anger'?"

"Well young man; this could be your lucky day. I was just about to call my daughter Doreen 'little Miss Anger herself' to tell her that her dad had a heart attack and is in the hospital. She won't be happy to get my call, because she doesn't care about him; as a matter of fact, as far as she's concerned, he's already dead. She's been consumed with hatred towards him since she was a little girl and then to make matters worse, he just walked out one day leaving us to fend for ourselves. She could never understand why he treated her so cruelly and I couldn't bring myself to tell her about his childhood and why he had so much anger and hurt inside of him."

She invited, "Let's go inside and I'll give her a call. I hope you don't mind but I won't tell her that you're here. She definitely won't come, if there is a stranger in the house. When she gets here, I'll say you're from the University, doing research on "Anger" for your master's degree."

The phone rang a few times and then a young girl's voice said, "Hello, I'm not available, you can leave a message but I probably won't get back to you."

"Hi Doreen, this is Mom; your father has been visiting me for the past week and today he had a heart attack and is not expected to live. Give me a call when you get this message."

Not even a half hour had passed before Jan heard someone coming in the front door. Doreen yelled out, "Mom where are you, are you okay?"

"I'm in the living honey and I'm fine!"

The first thing Doreen wanted to know was what "he" was doing here.

"Mom, did he hurt you?"

"He just came to see if we were okay."

"Did he say why it took him twenty years to find out where we lived?"

"I think you could show a little more concern; after all he is your father."

"Mom, we've been through all this before. I told you that he stopped being my father the first time I saw him lay a hand on you. I'm sure there'll be a time when I will forget what he did to you, but I'll never forgive him!"

"Doreen, he is lying in a hospital bed dying; so for your sake, I think you should forgive him. You have no idea what he went through as a child and I could never tell you, because it was too gruesome. Besides, you had so much hate for him that I didn't think it would make a difference."

"Well, you got that right, Mom, so let's not talk about it now."

"We need to talk and get everything out in the open."

"Mom, I've told you a thousand times, as far as I'm concerned, he's been dead for years."

"Please Doreen, just go to the hall closet and bring out the old brown suitcase; it's on the shelf next to the box of Christmas decorations."

Doreen turned around but stopped when she saw David sitting in the easy chair next to the big living room window.

"Who in the ... are you, and what are you doing in our house?"

Jan got up quickly and stood in front of Doreen and said, "This is David McMaster, he's from the University. I'm helping him with his Master's degree; it's on 'Anger;' as a matter of fact everyone on 'Anger Street' is assisting him. After all, he's one of us honey, he just lives down the street at No. 7."

"Anyway, just forget he's here honey; now please get the suitcase and let's talk."

Pointing to the closet Doreen commented, "Mom, I've been in that closet a thousand times and I have never seen a suitcase."

I know honey; but I knew you would come when I called, so I brought it down from my bedroom. I've kept it hidden all these years because I knew you wouldn't want to see it if you knew it belonged to your father. When he left he told me to put it in the garbage; he said it brought back too many bad memories."

When Doreen came back into the room, she looked at her mother and told her, "I don't want to do this; not now, not ever."

"Well, you're going to young lady. I should have shared this with you a long time ago, but I could never bring myself to tell you about your father's tragic life."

Opening the case, Jan took out an old Bible and handed it to Doreen, saying, "I want you to read what's written inside the front cover."

"Okay, I'll read it, but it won't change the way I feel."

Doreen started reading to herself, but Jan touched her hand and insisted, "Out loud please."

To my Darling Son Donny

I'm sorry I couldn't protect us from your Father and now I'm too tired and I have no fight left in me. I want you to promise me that you'll get as far away from your Father as you can. I pray that you will forgive me, so we can spend eternity with God in Heaven. Love Mom

Doreen closed the Bible and asked, "Mom, what does this have to do with Dad beating you all those years?"

"You need to understand that your father had a lot of anger in him and it got worse every time he remembered his dad hitting his mom. He had to leave us because he was becoming more and more like his Father every day."

"I'll tell you the story just like your Father told it to me."

One day when he arrived home from school, he found this Bible on his bed. When he read the writing inside, he started to cry and called out for his mom. He dropped the Bible on the bed and started running down the stairs calling out to her.

When she didn't answer, he started to panic. After searching every room in the house, he then ran out into the yard and through his tears, he kept calling for her. When he got to the two big wooden barn doors, he knew something was wrong because his mother would have come out as soon as she heard him calling.

Wiping his eyes on his sleeve, Donny slowly opened the barn door. When his eyes adjusted to the darkness, he saw his Mom hanging from one of the wooden beams. Falling to his knees, he kept saying over and over, "Mom, why did you leave me here all alone?"

He stayed on his knees until he heard his father's pickup truck entering the yard. Donny knew even before he went outside that his father would be "drunk as a skunk." Stumbling out of the truck and almost falling to the ground, he saw Donny standing there.

"What are you doing boy?" his father asked. Go and tell that no-good mother of yours that I'm home and I want my supper!"

Donny looked his father in the eye and said, "I guess you'll have to fix your own supper, Mom's gone away. This time she's finally rid of you."

"Don't talk to me in that tone of voice, you rotten kid; go tell your mother that I'm home." Donny pointed his finger and yelled, "Go tell her yourself; she's just hanging around in the barn!"

Doreen felt chills going up her spine as her mother continued to tell the story. "I think your dad lost his ability to show any emotion after that day.

Apparently he never left home like his mother asked him to. He stayed close by and watched his father slowly kill himself with alcohol."

Continuing, she shared, "I was shocked when your father told me he enjoyed watching his old man die. He said he spent every day sitting across from his Dad so he could keep him drunk out of his mind twenty-four hours a day.

When his father would get sick, your dad would pour him another glass of booze; if he said he didn't want any more, your father would hold his nose and force him to drink. Then with a big grin on his face, he would just sit there and watch his father cry out in pain."

"Your dad knew it was just a matter of time before the alcohol took its toll and he was determined to help speed up the process so he could get on with his life."

"One morning your Dad woke up early and looked over at his pitiful father sitting in the chair across from him.

When he didn't see any movement from the big fat belly, he smiled and looked down at the ugly twisted face of the man he hated saying, 'I hope you rot in hell you ... because that's what you deserve!'

Doreen had tears in her eyes as she held the Bible close to her chest. "Mom, I think I finally understand. Dad went away because he didn't want to hurt you anymore. Come on Mom, let's go to that little country Church so I can pray for Dad and then I want to go to the hospital and tell him that I love him and ask for his forgiveness."

David walked out of the house and stood on the veranda waiting for Jan and Doreen, but when they finally came out they just walked past him as if he wasn't even there.

"The Golden Bench"

Prayer is when we raise our hearts to God, and his spirit catches us, and begins to propel us where he is going. That is the biggest adventure you're ever going to have in your life. I've said before I believe the local church is the hope of the world. And if it's the hope of the world it's because of prayer.

You see, prayer is not the spiritual equivalent of the chess club. It's more like rugby. It's where the battle is fought and won. Prayer is what sends the Devil running. Prayer is what mobilizes God's people. Prayer is how we find out where God wants us to be in his grand adventure. Then things start to happen that are beyond all we could ask or even imagine according to the power that is propelling us, and we start to do things and go places that we never dreamed of before.

Story Four

Can Two Wrongs Ever Make A Right?

"If you become angry, do not let your anger lead you into sin, and do not stay angry all day." (Ephesians 4:26)

David rang the bell and then stood back and waited. He was a little surprised when he heard an older woman's voice call out; "Hold on, I'm coming!"

The door opened and there stood the sweetest little old lady that he had ever seen. Following right behind her was a mild mannered gentleman whom David guessed was her protector. The little man must have had problems with his eyesight, because he was standing right behind her, yet had to ask, "Who is it dear?"

She replied, "I don't know who he is, but he looks like a very nice young man!"

The old man offered David his hand and greeted him; "Hello, I'm Danny Stone and this is my wife Rebecca. How may we help you?"

"Nice to meet you Sir, my name is David McMaster and I'm just passing through the neighborhood doing a survey on 'Anger.'

Mrs. Stone pointed her little finger at David and remarked, "You can't fool me young man; I know you; you moved in next door at # 6 about a month ago. We haven't seen very much of you; I guess you work long hours."

"I'm sorry Mrs. Stone but you must be mistaken. You see ma'am, I just arrived here today and I will be moving on before it gets dark. I've heard that everyone has a double, but I pity the poor guy that looks like me."

"Please come in young man and we will sit and talk. Why don't you and Danny go into the living room and I'll bring some hot tea and cookies."

David looked around the room and commented, "You have a lovely home, Sir, and I can tell by the smell of homemade bread that your wife must be a great cook!"

"She's the best in the world and if you had met our son Jerry, you would have seen the results of her cooking. He was 6'4" and topped the scales at around 250 pounds."

"Boy, he sure was a big man! I pity any guy who would make him 'Angry.'

From the look on Danny's face, David knew that he had said the wrong thing. He tried to change the subject, but couldn't find the right words.

At that moment, Rebecca returned carrying a tray. Her warm smile lit up the whole room. "What are you two talking about?"

They just looked at each other but didn't utter a word. Rebecca smiled and said, "I know you two were talking about my Jerry, right? David, did Danny show you Jerry's picture? I love this one, it's my favorite. I think he looks so handsome in his uniform; don't you agree?"

"Oh yes, I agree with you! Was he in the army?"

"No," Rebecca replied; "He was a Marine, a Green Beret. He went to Viet Nam, but he never came home. We got a letter from the military saying something about him being MIA. They even sent us a metal, I believe it represents bravery; I'm sure it's around here somewhere."

"Anyway, we didn't pay any attention to what they were saying. We know our Jerry is alive and well. I think the little rascal found himself a cute little Asian girl and has settled down in some small town. I expect him home any day now. You see, Sir, I'm dying to see my grandchildren. I wonder if they can speak English, because at my age I don't think I could learn another language. Lately I have enough trouble just speaking English."

Danny interrupted, suggesting, "Honey, why don't you get David and I some of those delicious brownies you made the other day?"

"Sorry Danny, but if you remember, I put them in the freezer so it will take quite a while to thaw them out."

"We don't mind waiting. You know what I always say, 'anything worth having is worth waiting for', right David?"

"Yes Sir, I agree wholeheartedly!"

When Rebecca left the room, Danny turned to David; "As you can see my dear wife can't or won't accept our son's death. She even blocks out the real reason he went into the service in the first place.

If it's okay with you David, I would like to tell you Jerry's story."

"Please Danny, go ahead; I want to know everything.

"We used to live on a small farm out west; it wasn't much, but we got by. Of course there was always a lot of work for Rebecca and me, so it was such a blessing when Jerry came along to help us out.

We could tell, even when he was a young boy that he would grow up to be a fine young man and be as strong as an ox."

"When Jerry started school, all the kids made fun of him because of his size. To make matters worse, the maintenance man had to make him a special desk that was so big; the only place it would fit was in a corner away from the other kids."

Danny's story continued; "As the years passed, Jerry grew bigger and taller so of course the teasing at school continued to get worse. At least one day a week, Jerry would come home from school early. He would tell us that the principal suspended him again for fighting and not just with one kid; oh no, not our boy! He had to take on two or three of them at one time."

"The only time Jerry acted meek and mild was when he was with his girlfriend Tina. He loved her more than life and all he ever talked about was marrying her and having lots of children. Actually, Tina did most of the talking and Jerry just listened and nodded his head in approval."

"One beautiful summer day, just after his eighteenth birthday, Jerry told his mother and me that he was going to the big city to make his fortune and once he did, he would come home and marry his beautiful Tina!"

"He was only gone about two months when we had to call him and tell him that something terrible had happened to his sweetheart. The phone went silent for a moment and then in a worried voice Jerry promised, 'Dad I'll be home in a few days," and then he hung up.

"Jerry arrived home sooner than he had planned and the first thing he said was, 'I want to see Tina, where is she?'"

"Jerry, there is something I need to tell you; your Tina is not the same person you knew before you left. You see son, she was raped by a bunch of guys and the doctor thinks it did something to her mind."

"Please Dad; I just want to see her!"

"When Jerry walked into the hospital room, he couldn't believe his eyes. His beautiful Tina was lying on the bed but she wasn't the same person he knew when he went off to fight in the war. He barely recognized her; it was like someone else was in the bed pretending to be her."

"Her beautiful hair was a tangled mess and her eyes were almost closed due to the swelling. Jerry could see that her jaw was broken and when he spoke to her, she didn't respond and that was the last straw. Through clinched teeth and tightened fists he made a vow to his fiancée, insisting, 'I promise you, my darling that the men who hurt you will pay with their lives!'

"His Dad grabbed his arm and implored, "Please Jerry, let the Police handle this; you know it would kill your mother if anything happened to you."

"Just tell Mom I'll be okay and that I'll be home as soon as I take care of a little business."

Jerry went directly to the police station and asked who was in charge of the Tina Miller case. The officer at the desk replied, "That would be Sergeant Connors. Please wait here and I'll see if he is busy."

After about five minutes, a plain clothes officer came out and said, "Hi, I'm Sergeant Connors and you are?"

"I'm Jerry, Jerry Stone; Tina's boyfriend."

"Please come into my office and I'll fill you in on the latest information we have. I'm sorry my friend, but we don't have much to go on because we haven't been able to get Tina's side of the story."

"Have you rounded-up any suspects or gangs in the area?"

"No not really, but we have talked to some of the local boys; they didn't know anything. There's a good possibility that some punks were just passing through our little town and decided to stir up some trouble."

The Sergeant then looked at Jerry and said, "I think you should go home and be with your family. I'll contact you if we get any new leads."

Jerry returned the look and replied, "I'm sure you will, but I want to make one thing clear; you better find them before I do, because I've got nothing to lose!"

When he was a young boy, Jerry taught himself to hunt and fish and he was also an excellent woodsman, spending days and sometimes a whole week living off the land and enjoying Mother Nature. This made him very familiar with the area where his sweetheart was attacked.

He started spending many hours looking for clues that would identify the gang members. There was one spot near the lake where he noticed a fireplace made out of rocks and thought, "This is definitely a party place;" but when he checked out the surrounding area, he was a little confused, because there weren't any footprints. He didn't have to look very hard to find the big branch that someone had used to cover their tracks to deter people from knowing someone had been partying there.

Another thing that caught Jerry's eye was a pile of empty beer cans; when he sorted through them he noticed that every fifth or sixth can was crushed, indicating that someone was very angry.

The next day, Jerry asked his dad to help him carry his old wooden boat down to the lake, but he didn't tell him why. Although the police didn't think that Tina was attacked by locals, Jerry did; he was certain that if these guys believed they got away with this crime, they might be arrogant enough to keep on partying and looking for their next victim.

After patrolling the lake for two weeks, Jerry was getting very disappointed because he couldn't find any new clues and the trail was getting cold.

Then one sunny afternoon while he was fishing near a small cove, he heard music playing and people singing out of tune. As he rounded the bend, he could see the hidden cove and a beach with about six young men attempting to dance but they were so drunk they could hardly stand up.

When Jerry brought his boat to the shoreline, one of the drunks shouted, "Hey you, this is a private party so get lost!"

Jerry yelled back, "Don't worry about me, I'll be gone in a few minutes. My boat has a small leak and all I want to do is empty out some of the water, then I'll be on my way."

Just then another guy who looked like he hadn't taken a bath in weeks confronted Jerry ordering, "Make it quick or you'll be one sorry guy!"

After a loud burp the drunk finished his beer, and then crushed the can; with a smile that showed his rotten teeth and then tossed the can into Jerry's boat. Jerry could feel the anger building up inside of him as he stared at the crushed can.

Wordlessly, he reached into the boat and took out a huge axe handle; he started to walk toward old dirty face that was now laughing hysterically and calling to his buddies to come and watch him kick the crap out of this loser.

"Come on boys, let's show this guy how real men party!"

The guy on Jerry's left side took a swing, but he was so drunk he missed by a mile. Reacting quickly Jerry swung the axe handle and the sound of the wood hitting the guy's head could be heard over the loud music.

It was a sickening sound that made all the guys stop in their tracks. They may have stopped, but Jerry didn't. He hit the next guy across his knees and he crashed down, letting out a piercing painful cry. The other three guys begged Jerry to stop, but he continued beating them until the last one fell to the ground, leaving only the man with the rotten teeth to face his punishment.

Jerry swung the bat at the guy's head but missed him on purpose; the guy fell on the ground and with a look of panic cried, "Why are you attacking us? What did we ever do to you?"

"It's not what you did to me, it's what you did to the woman I love. We were going to be married next year but that won't happen because of what you guys did to her and for that you will pay dearly!"

"What are you talking about, you nut bar?"

"Do you remember a few weeks ago when you and your friends were partying and you saw a pretty young girl all alone on the beach? You knew she wouldn't put up much of a fight so the six of you decided to have a little fun and take turns raping her."

"I swear Mister, it wasn't me! I never touched her; it was Freddie and the other guys. I tried to stop them but they wouldn't listen, you gotta believe me!"

Jerry pointed the axe handle and said to the coward lying on the ground crying; "You listen to me; you piece of trash! In my eyes you're all guilty and I'm going to make sure each of you pay for putting my Tina in a mental hospital."

He added, "I know my Tina wasn't your first victim, but I'll make sure today that she's your last. By the way, her last name is Miller and she was going to change it to Stone, but you never gave her the chance."

The guy started to say something, but Jerry didn't let him speak; he just kept on hitting him until his arms and legs were broken. He was just about to deliver the final blow to the man's head when he heard a voice behind him call out, "Attention, this is the police! Put down that weapon and back away!"

Jerry dropped the axe handle and turned to face Sergeant Connors, who had stopped to check each of the bodies to determine if they were dead or alive.

"I hope you made sure these are the right guys, Mr. Stone; if not you're in a lot of trouble."

"Oh, it's them alright and this poor excuse for a man is their ringleader; but take it from me Sir; they're all guilty. I'm sure you won't have any trouble getting them to confess."

Mr. Stone looked at David and said, "Things were never the same around here after what happened; they put poor Tina in a mental institution and Jerry joined the marines. We received some letters and pictures from him for a while but then he was sent to Viet Nam and we never heard from him again."

Just then Rebecca returned to the room carrying a tray and as she laid it on the table she commented, "I hope you guys are ready to eat the best brownies on Anger Street!" Sitting down and patting David's knee, she looked at her husband and said, "Isn't it nice having Jerry home again, Papa?"

David just sat there thinking, "Anger can destroy people's lives and leave scars that never go away," and then he thought of a passage from the Bible:

Stop 'for I know the plans I have for you," says the Lord. "They are plans for good and not for disaster, to give you a future and a hope.

Jeremiah 29:11

When David got outside he went to the "The Golden Bench" just on the other side of the picket fence. He picked up the piece of paper lying there, and began to read:

After He heard about His friend, John the Baptist, He withdrew to a deserted place by Himself. After He fed the five thousand, where there was a rush of ministry success, we are told he "went up the mountain by Himself to pray."

Luke speaks about this in a way that implies there's a regular practice going on here:

> *Jesus would withdraw to deserted places and pray. "Luke 5:16"*

He teaches His disciples to do the same thing. This is solitude.

Story Five

Angels Among Us

"Danny, are you ready? We're leaving in twenty minutes. His Mother waited a few minutes and then repeated her question.

Debbie Murphy was never one to lose her cool, especially with her two kids, but this time she felt she had to put her foot down and get everyone to cooperate if this "once a year" vacation was to be a success.

She knew as she climbed the long flight of stairs that she would find her youngest child, Kimberly or Angel as everyone called her, sitting on the floor in front of her big brother's bedroom. Stopping just before she reached the top step because she felt tears building up inside as she thought back to that night when her daughter was born and a few days later the love of her life went to be with our Lord.

She remembered how her wonderful childhood sweetheart had leaned over and kissed his sleeping "Angel" and then he made her a promise that he would be back in two days to bring her and her Mother home. But that wasn't to be: the plane that her man George boarded just a few hours later wouldn't make it to its destination and neither would the other seventy-nine passengers aboard flight 777.

Debbie continued her climb and sure enough, there was "Angel sitting on the floor, banging on her brother's door with her book of bedtime stories. Debbie put a big smile on her face as she walked down the hall.

As she reached down to pick up her crying baby girl, she whispered: that big brother of yours is going to get a licking and you can hold him while I give him a spanking. Oh no Mommy, please don't hurt him; he's the only brother I have.

Kissing "Angel" she said, okay not this time, but... she didn't get a chance to finish speaking because Danny's door opened and a spaceman with wires hanging from his body brushed by her and disappeared into another room across the hall.

Debbie looked at "Angel," and shaking her head said; what was that? Did you see that alien go by? That was not an alien Mommy. That was my brother Danny.

When he came out of the room, Danny gave them both a look; why are you knocking at my door? "Angel" put up her arms for Danny to take her, but he just squeezed her hand and started walking back into his room.

His Mom moved back and blocked the doorway and in a stern voice asked Danny if he remembered what was happening today? I know, Mom, its Saturday morning and I'm talking to my friends.

Debbie started to get a little annoyed at him, but caught herself in time and with a fake smile reminded him that this was the first day of their holidays. We've been talking about this vacation for over a month now; don't you ever listen? Yes, Mom, but I thought we were going next week, right now Mom, I need to get back to my computer. Kevin and I are working on a project. You listen to me young man: you are going into your room right this minute and sign off and shut down all of your projects and meet us at the front door in twenty minutes: is that clear?

Debbie didn't wait for an answer and as she walked down the hall with "Angel" her voice trailed off and Danny could hear her saying that they were going to have so much fun and it would be the best vacation ever.

It was going to be a long drive because this would be the first vacation the family would take with the new head of the clan. Although Doug and Debbie had been dating for about two years, it had only been six months since they got married. "Angel" accepted her new step Dad right away, but Danny thought his Mom was being selfish and unfaithful to his Father and that Doug was an imposter. One night at dinner, just before the wedding, Danny stormed out saying as he pointed to Doug; you'll never be my Father and you will never take his place. Debbie tried many times to talk to Danny about their new life, but he would not listen. I don't care, Mom if he is a Minister or a Preacher and I will not go to church anymore, because I do not believe in God; he took Dad away from me, so if he doesn't care about me, I don't care about him.

Nobody talked much during the trip. Debbie tried to start some conversations, but when she didn't get any response, she gave up and just lost herself in her new book called "Angels among us."

The mood and the tension around the campfire were no better than at home. Danny was not into nature so that put a damper on enjoying any outdoor activities.

One morning, Debbie suggested that they should all take a walk in the woods and look for some mushrooms, but when the campsite was tidied up after breakfast; Danny just went inside his tent and closed the flap. Debbie tried to keep her cool as she tried to persuade her Son to come with the family and they could have some fun together. Mom, I just want to be left alone. Well, that was the last straw and Debbie got mad, opened up the zipper and demanded that Danny come out now. He came out with his cell phone to his ear and that made his Mother even madder. Grabbing his arm, she pulled the phone from his hand. Without putting the phone to her ear, she spoke sharply: Danny can't come to the phone right now: he'll call you later and then she pushed the off button.

Rage was building up in Danny's face and he could hardly talk as he lashed out at his Mother: I hate you and I don't want to be part of this family anymore.

When he started running away, Debbie tried to stop him, but Doug grabbed her and told her that Danny needs to be alone to think things over; I'm not sure that he will be back anytime soon and besides, it will soon be lunchtime and you know he never likes to miss a meal.

It seemed like only a few minutes had passed and Debbie asked Doug where "Angel" was; she is not at the table? Panic set in when they checked the tents and the surrounding areas. Debbie felt like she was going out of her mind as she ran through the bushes, calling out for her little girl.

Doug was a little calmer and went to their van and on the ticket was an emergency phone number and within a few minutes, a truck with two park rangers were there and were ready to help.

Debbie was a mess and couldn't control herself, but thank God, Doug was able to tell the park staff what had happened so they could start the search.

Through his tears, Danny could hear "Angel's voice and it was so clear that he knew she must have been very close to him. He only had to walk a few feet and when he moved a low hanging branch, there in a small clearing was "Angel." She was sitting on a log and talking to someone.

Danny couldn't make out who it was because the sun was shining in his eyes. A big smile came on his face when he saw who she was talking to. It was their Father. Kneeling down beside "Angel," Danny couldn't say a word. He just stared and listened to every word.

Danny, you need to be a strong young man. Your mother and sister need you and you need them. Your mother didn't get married again just for herself. She knows that you and "Angel" need a father figure, someone to help both of you on your journey through life. God loves you very much and he sent someone to take my place. He didn't send someone to replace me.

I have to go know, but please promise me that you will look after your mother and your little sister and remember, I will be waiting for the day that we will all be together again.

Danny felt different as he watched his father slowly disappear. When he took "Angel's" hand, she asked him if they would see their Daddy again soon. We may not see him, but I know he will always be with us. Come on, let's hurry, because I'm sure Mom and Dad are worried about us.

Story Six

Sin City

After a short rest, David got to his feet and in the distance noticed a sign but could only discern the larger words that said: WELCOME TO SIN CITY; he gathered his strength and will-power and sprinted down the road. It wasn't until he was within a few feet that he could read the small print:

WELCOME TO

SIN CITY

NOTICE

It is highly recommended that you "Do Not" enter here; because you may not be able to return to the main road and you could spend "Eternity" in this God-forsaken place.

After reading the sign, David noticed that many of his fellow travelers gladly entered the exit without looking back. The few that did talk to him queried, "What's wrong with you? You have a chance to rid yourself of your burdens, so come on; you'd be crazy to pass up a great opportunity like this!"

He sighed as he felt the weight of his luggage shift places once again. David was sure they were putting on weight, because they felt heavier by the minute.

Being a business man, David was aware that making the right choices at the right time could determine whether he would win or lose.

But as he thought about his present situation, he knew he could either continue on the road carrying his burdens or join his fellow travelers in restorative rest and recuperation. It didn't require much thought and besides, as far as he was concerned, he'd live his life however he chose to live it.

His mind was definitely made up when he looked down the road called "Grief" and saw people struggling to keep going, while this rest stop looked so sunny and bright. Without further thought, David joined the line to the exit ramp. He did notice one thing: the exit lane was one way only.

There was a road leading back to the main highway, but it was covered with bushes growing through its cracked pavement. It was obvious to David that the road was not used very much, so that's why it didn't require ongoing maintenance.

He decided if he didn't like this place, he could leave any time he wanted to by just following the unused road back to where he started. He did notice another good thing: his load was getting lighter the further he veered off the main highway.

Someone behind David shouted, "Hey! What is going on up at the front of the line? I can hear people laughing and having fun; let's keep the line moving!"

David was so tall that he could see over the heads of everyone in the line in front of him. Without turning around, he said out loud, "I see a circus and lots of signs, but I can't make out what the people are saying. The line is starting to move faster, you'll get there soon enough."

When David reached the front of the line, he started smiling; something that he hadn't done since he started his journey. "Step right up!" the man in the bright colored coat shouted as he took off his roaring twenties, white straw hat. Making a swooping gesture, he invited David to enter through the archway.

"Welcome my friend, your troubles are over. From now on, you will be living the life you were meant to live, without worries or burdens; just partying with your friends 24 hours a day. You don't even need money, everything is free!"

David looked at the guy and questioned, "What if I get tired of all of this and I want to leave?"

"Oh! You'll never want to leave this place, but if you do, you will join that line over there."

"What line? I don't see anybody."

"Exactly, nobody ever leaves here; it's a place where dreams come true!"

The smiling man asked, "Well my friend, do you want to enter?"

Just then someone behind David interjected, "Come on; if you don't want to go in, get out of the way and give us a chance to enter."

David thought for a second and then started walking forward. "Hold it there sir; you'll have to drop off your two traveling companions; I mean your two burdens; they don't get to go in, so you'll be rid of them for good."

The two dwarfs climbed down off of David's back and with tears in their eyes, they held up their signs "Loneliness and Denial" and said to David, "Are you sure you want to leave us here?"

"Well, you guys were getting very heavy and besides, the man promised that I can go in and hook up with you guys later."

Just before David stepped into the arch, he heard a commotion to his left. A man who looked like a wine-o was trying to get to David. He was screaming, "Don't come in, it's a trap. I once had the world at my feet and look at me now; this will happen to you. Take warning my friend; you'll never get out of here alive!"

Two men in uniform grabbed the drunk and started to drag him away. He was staring directly at David and trying to signal him to look at the back of the two security guards. David didn't know if it was the lights or all the excitement going on, but he thought he could see tails and wings on the guards.

He shook his head and when he looked back in their direction, they were gone. The guy with the hat motioned him to move along. "Welcome traveler," were the last words David heard as he was gently pushed forward.

Once inside, David couldn't believe his eyes. Nothing he could dream up compared to what he was seeing; not even Vegas. "I need to go slow, I'll just have a little fun and then I will be on my way."

There were so many things to do but it didn't matter what he chose, because everything was free.

He looked at the different names on the hotels, places like Greed, Corruption, Loser, Bad News, and of course old faithful, Heartbreak Hotel.

David chose a local bar called "Revenge." Although he had never been in a place like this before, he was sure from the way he was greeted at the front door by the two lovely ladies dressed in their sixties outfits, that he was going to feel right at home. Everyone in the room greeted him like a long lost brother.

David could usually hold his own when it came to drinking, but he wanted to keep his wits about him, so he told the waitress to bring him a soda. "I'm sorry sir," the waitress said; "the only way you can get a soda in here is in a mixed drink. You know: a rum and coke, rye and ginger..."

"Fine, I'll have a beer."

"What size?" asked the waitress, as she stood there chewing gum. "We have large, extra-large, and super-large and of course we have the one that all the real men order called "two hands Nelly."

You don't look like much of a drinker, so maybe you should start with a large; or maybe you can only handle a woman's drink like a "pink pussycat" or would that be too much for a big man like you?"

With everyone staring at David he said, "I'll have an extra-large beer."

The waitress patted his head and said, "Coming right up." Everyone could hear her call out to the bartender, "Hey Charlie; we got a live wire on table 13!"

There was a steady line up of people waiting to sit and talk to the new guy, but it was the ladies that wanted to be close to this big handsome man.

The time passed by quickly and before David realized it, the bartender was hollering out, "Last call; last call to the bar."

David ordered one more, but before he could finish it the waitress took it off the table and warned, "We're closing now sir but we open again at 6:00AM. You have to be out of here in five minutes."

When David stepped outside, he found himself in a cold, dark place that looked like a compound surrounded by big stone walls. He turned to go back into the bar but he couldn't find the door; it had turned into a solid wall.

When his eyes adjusted to the darkness, David could see that someone had lit a few fires. He made his way to the one that was closest to him, where he saw four or five guys standing around an oil barrel. The flame didn't give off much light and even less heat. David pulled up the collar on his coat and stepped closer to the small flame.

After saying "hello" a few times, he tried to get between two of the men so at least the front of his body would feel a little warmer.

Nobody moved to let him in so all he could do was put his hand through a space where two bodies came together. "I can't stay here like this until the morning," he thought. "I need to find some place warm so I can get some sleep." David got even colder the further he was from the fire.

The night was dark, but David could still make out forms. He could even see people lying down, although he couldn't tell if it was a man or a woman. After what seemed like hours, David heard a woman's voice say, "I'll share my blanket for a drink of whatever you have."

David hesitated for a moment, but then decided to move on. He was going to say, "I don't have anything to drink," but that would have only been half of the reason why he wouldn't lay with this woman.

His Emily wouldn't approve, well actually, she would kill him if she found out. Then he realized, "she's not here; she's gone and I can do whatever I want."

But, he knew in his heart that it wouldn't be right to be with someone else and how would he explain himself if there was a "Heaven" and he met her there.

He shook his head and reminded himself, "I guess where I'm going there is not much chance of seeing any of my friends, let alone my precious Emily."

Not watching where he was going, David tripped over someone and landed on the ground in a pile of garbage; or at least it smelled like garbage. Feeling around, he did manage to find some papers, maybe newspapers.

It didn't matter because once he put some over his cold shaking body, using a few more as a pillow, he soon drifted off to sleep. It was not a good sleep, maybe closer to a nightmare; a nightmare that would haunt him every time he closed his eyes.

The bright light of the sun stirred David from his restless sleep. After rubbing his eyes, he got his first sight of his sleeping quarters. To his surprise, what he thought was a garbage dump was actually a barnyard and his newspaper pillow was some old dirty hay. He kept wondering how he got from a big bustling city to a farm in the country.

A voice broke through the silence questioning, "Who are you and what are you doing on my property? I have a shotgun with a load of buckshot, and it's got your name on it; so if you don't want to leave this world in several pieces, you had better get your butt out of here!"

David arose slowly and without looking at the man or his gun, he quickly left the farm and headed down the road, but to where he did not know.

After walking for a short time, David sat down on a big rock and closed his eyes. He quickly opened them when he heard a voice ask, "You going into town, Mister?"

David shook his head, confirming the question without talking.

"You'll have to ride in the back with Mable."

As he climbed into the back of the wagon, he was face-to-face with the largest pig he had ever seen! Not that he had ever seen a real live pig before, only in pictures; but he once attended a BBQ where they were roasting one.

"Here's your stop," the driver stated as he slowed down and then stopped in front of the gates to "Sin City." David thanked the driver as the old creaking wagon lumbered out of sight.

David was hungry and his body needed food, but strangely enough his mind was telling him he needed a drink more than food. David couldn't imagine wanting a drink this early in the morning or at any time of the day, for that matter.

He saw the sign "Revenge Hotel" then said to himself, "I had a good time there even though they closed early; maybe they will stay open later tonight."

With a big smile David walked into the hotel but was stopped at the door by a heavy-set bouncer. "Buddy, you smell like a pig, so you can't come in here. I won't have you upsetting our fine clientele; go find yourself another place to drink."

After trying four or five more places, David was ready to give up, but then he saw a rundown building with a little sign that read, "Rejects Tavern; we serve everyone, even you.:

The place looked like it had been condemned by the board of health, but David couldn't find the sign. After stepping over a few drunken bodies, he found a place to sit at an empty table near the bar.

The scar faced bartender grumbled, "What are you drinking Sir," as he spit on a glass before wiping it with a dirty cloth. He didn't direct the request to anyone in particular, but David knew he was talking to him.

With a very dry voice, David ordered two beers and a shot.

The "Reject's Tavern" became David's home during drinking hours. Because of the way he looked and smelled, this was the only drinking spot in town that would serve him.

The more David drank, the more he looked like the town drunk. The only time he had a clear head was in the morning just before he started drinking. But even then his mind was far from crystal clear.

One morning on his way to his favorite drinking spot, David decided to take a detour. The sun was shining and it was warm and he didn't feel like sitting in that dingy low life cesspool.

Sitting on the sidewalk, deep in thought, David heard a gentle voice behind him asking, "Do you need a friend?"

When he turned around he saw an old man sitting in a doorway. Confused David asked, "Are you talking to me?"

"Yes I am son and I know what you're going through. I've been where you are; as a matter of fact, I'm still there. I can also tell by the way you look that Sin City is not what you thought it would be.

I'm sure you've asked yourself a thousand times, how did I ever get this low and will I ever escape from this place?"

The old man motioned for David to come closer. But, because he was still drunk from the night before David was having trouble getting to his feet. After trying a few times with no success, he decided to crawl over to where the old man had his cardboard house. Seeing him lying there in his box, David thought, "This man lives like a turtle, he carries his house with him!"

In a very soft voice the old man confided to David, "There is a way out, but I'm not sure you have what it takes to get back on the road called Grief."

"I'm listening old-timer, what do I have to do?"

"Well my friend, you have to reach bottom. You might think you're already there, but you're not. You're close, but you have a ways to go. Come with me and I will show you the way."

"Why not; I'm not doing anything else right now and besides, my chauffeur's late, so I've got some time to kill!"

Standing up, the old man moved a few boxes out of the way and as he opened a big wooden door he motioned for David to follow him.

It was so dark inside that David could hardly see, but he did hear the old man warning, "Watch your step."

"I need you to stay close to me, because there are a lot of holes in the floor and if you fall into one of them, you won't be coming out! Also keep close to the wall and you should be okay."

When David's eyes adjusted to the darkness it was like that first night in the compound; he could see shapes, but didn't know what they were.

After going through a few rooms, he caught up with the old man who was standing in front of a mirror. When he stood next to his new friend, David realized that they were looking through one of those two-way mirrors.

Suddenly, a woman came up and put her face very close to the mirror. She was checking her make-up while running her fingers through her hair.

David jumped back and gave a little yell, like a little boy who was caught with his hand in the cookie jar. It only took a second for him to realize that the women couldn't see him.

Stepping a little closer, David's blood ran cold as he looked into the ugliest face he had ever seen. It was a face that could only belong to a creature from hell.

The old man grabbed David's arm and warned, "She's not the only creature from down below. Take a close look at all the staff and those hotel patrons with their backs against the wall and you'll see that they're all demons; even the hotel itself is a product of Satan. I guess you could say the whole place is a stopover, on the road to damnation!"

Pointing to a waitress serving one of the tables the old man remarked, "Check out her back; you'll notice that when she is facing a customer she looks normal, but the view from behind shows who she really is: one of the Devil's Disciples."

Letting out a sigh, David stepped back from the mirror. The old man put his hand on his back and commiserated, "Don't feel bad about having been deceived; you're not the first and you won't be the last. I've seen thousands of good people who couldn't handle life's hardships turn to alcohol and drugs and that's when they end up in a place like this. The Devil holds the franchise for these kinds of hell-holes. Even if he charged admission, there would be a very long lineup every night."

He continued, "Nobody ever starts out saying, boy I can't wait to become an alcoholic so I can lose my family, my friends, my job and my self-respect and then go someplace and die a lonely painful death.

Son, I know you've heard it many times before, but I'll say it again, *life is about choices*. The ones you make today will determine the life you'll live tomorrow."

David turned to the old man and declared, "I've seen enough! What do I have to do to get out of this place?"

"Well I don't know for sure, but I'm guessing you're not a Christian, but you probably believe in God; am I right?"

David nodded his head in agreement. He was just about to add that if his wife Emily had anything to do with it; he would have been a Deacon or a Minister. But he remained silent as he remembered that she was no longer in his world. It was time for David to face the fact that if he was going to make it through all of this, he had to turn to someone and who better than God?

"Are you okay?" his new friend enquired.

"Yes! I was just thinking about someone, someone very special to me."

David broke down as he told his new friend about the love of his life and how much he missed her. With tears filling his eyes and clenching his fist he stated, "I know Emily would want me to fight and not just give up when the going got a little rough.

She never backed down from anything or anyone, including me, and she was only half my size!"

The elderly man replied, "I had me a woman once, only she was meaner than a junk yard dog and could drink any four men under the table!"

"Enough reminiscing David; we have to move quickly as you don't have a lot of time. I know you're not going to like this, but the only way out of here is through the *Swamp of Filth*. However, there is one little problem; you will be up to your neck in the slime and just when all hope is gone and you're going down, you need to call out to the Lord; only then will He take your hand and lead you to safety."

"Is that all there is?"

"Yes, but because I have never had the guts to go through the ordeal, I don't know if it works. But then again, you don't have any other option."

David thought for a moment, then standing tall he asked, "How do I get to the cesspool?"

"I have a place where you can get cleaned up, and then you must go to the hotel called *Sinner's Paradise*. Once there you must sit at the end of the bar next to the kitchen. That's where you'll find the entrance to the *Swamp of Filth*.

After getting cleaned up, David asked, "Is there anything else I need to know?"

"Yes, there is one more thing."

The old man came right up to David and told him, "You're going to have to drink without getting so drunk that you can't remember where you are."

"Why do I have to get drunk?" David wanted to know.

"Because they won't let you in if they think you are going to try to escape. They know all the tricks; their master the Devil has taught them well!"

"Remember, you have to wait until the last minute to call upon God. Good luck my friend, I wish I was going with you, but I guess it is not meant to be."

Standing at the front door David looked up at the hotel sign *Sinner's Paradise* and remarked aloud, "I'm doing this for Emily. I know she's in heaven with her God and maybe she will put in a good word for me."

"Good afternoon Sir, table for one?"

"No thanks, I'll just sit at the bar for a while."

"Make your way to the far side of the room and the man with the big smile will be happy to serve you."

The room was crowded, but David saw an empty stool at the bar. Some people sitting at a big table tried to talk to him, but he just smiled and kept on going. Just before he got to the stool, a man in a checkered jacket sat down and in a loud voice tried to pick up a blond girl who was clearly not interested in what he had to say.

Avoiding the drunk, the blond turned to talk to someone at a nearby table and David got a glimpse of her back in the mirror. Letting out a little "wow", he could see that she was *one of them*.

With a quick turn she faced David, smiled, and then motioned for the doorman to remove the unwanted drunk from her area. Even looking through blurred eyes the obnoxious little man could see that he was no match for the enormous bouncer, so he just slithered away.

Sitting on the stool David said, "I'll have a large beer."

"Coming right up Sir," was the bartender's reply. After taking a glass from the shelf he inspected it to make sure it was clean. The now-smiling blond beside him questioned, "Don't I know you? Weren't you in here last week?"

David responded, "No, I'm new in town."

She just smiled, and then turned to talk to the guy on the other side of her.

David didn't know how much he could drink and still pull off his plan. He assumed he would soon find out, because the bartender was bringing him a very, very large beer!

The place stayed lively with everyone singing and dancing, so no one was paying any attention to the quiet guy at the end of the bar.

When David saw that the bartender was busy, he took the opportunity to check out the dark hallway leading to the kitchen. He couldn't see much because it was so dark. What he did notice was that nobody was going in or coming out of the kitchen, even though there was food on every table.

David was worried that the place might close before he could get through the passageway. He had to know what was down that hallway so he picked an olive from the bar and threw it towards the kitchen. To his surprise, it just hung there in midair and then slowly disappeared into what looked like thick syrup.

Next, he tossed an ashtray which did the same thing. David knew that this was the doorway he needed to go through but he needed to make his move when no one was watching.

Pretending to drop something on the floor, David slid off the stool and while he was on his knees he put his hand through the liquid. It felt like water only thicker. He had trouble getting his arm out once the liquid was up to his elbows. It was like something was pulling him in. It had a good grip on him so he had to use all his strength to release his arm.

Kneeling on the floor and looking at his arm to see if it was okay David heard someone ask him, "What are you doing down there?"

He looked up and saw the drunk in the checkered coat. When he said, "I lost something," the drunk replied, "Do you need any help?"

"No, I'm okay, but thanks anyway."

"Would you like me to call the waitress?"

"No, no, I'm fine! You just go on and enjoy yourself."

David was trying to get rid of the drunk before he drew attention to what he was doing. To prove that he was inebriated, David staggered a few times before trying to get on the bar stool. In a loud voice, he ordered another beer. David started to panic when he realized it was getting close to closing time.

He needed to act fast or he would lose his one and only chance to freedom. He knew luck was on his side when he looked toward the far side of the room where the drunk with the checkered coat was causing trouble. Looking around, he noted that everyone was watching the drunk, but to his amazement he saw that the guy was not drunk at all; he was just pretending. Things really got out of hand when the guy pulled out a cross and started preaching.

The devil's demons were moving in around the man with the cross and they weren't attempting to disguise themselves. Their long tails were swinging around and their wings were flapping. David wasn't about to stick around to see what they were going to do to this poor guy.

He jumped off the stool and stood in front of the invisible liquid wall. Putting his two hands out in front of him, he watched them disappear. If David had any doubts about entering the dark world, it was too late. There was some kind of force drawing him in!

Just before his head went in, he took a deep breath, not knowing how long he would be immersed in the liquid before he got to the other side. He didn't have to wait long; it was just like passing through a doorway from one room to the next.

Only this was not a room, it was a swamp. David found himself standing on a hill overlooking a dead world.

He could see small fires and trees with only their black trunks sticking out of the slime. What grabbed David's attention the most was the rancid smell. It was the same smell as the compound and the *Reject Hotel*! It was the stench of vomit and it took David's breath away.

All of a sudden, the ground gave away and David started sliding down a hill. He was in a panic because he knew what was at the bottom to greet him.

He was expecting to hear a splash when he entered the *Swamp of Filth*, but it wasn't liquid like water it was thick like quicksand. The slime was up to his waist and he was sinking fast! He knew that if he didn't call out to God at the right moment, he would surely die.

Before he knew it the slime was up to his neck. He started calling out to God; "I know I have turned away from you in the past, but now I am imploring you to help me get out of this hell!"

Unable to move his arms and with the vile liquid only a few inches away from his mouth, David gave up. He closed his eyes imploring; "I love you Emily and I love you God!"

Then everything went black. The next thing he knew he was standing on the road called "Grief" with his two little companions on his back. Someone behind him asked impatiently, "Are you taking this exit or not?"

David looked at the guy and advised, "No I'm not and I don't think you should either."

However, the man just pushed him aside and mumbled something about enjoying the good things in life.

Story Seven

The Anniversary

"Hurry up honey, the limo will be here in twenty minutes and they charge extra if we make them wait!"

Cindy stuck her head out of the bathroom door and hollered, "What are you going to do if it takes me another hour? Maybe you're planning on going without me?"

Ronnie just shook his head and out loud he said, "It's the same every year."

Then he heard Cindy's voice again, "I'm listening sweetheart; what did you say?"

With a little smile Ronnie hollered back, "I said, I can't wait to have a beer." This time, Cindy came out of the bathroom and with her hands on her hips; she gave Ronnie a look that made his blood run cold.

As he backed out of the bedroom, he smiled and said, "Don't worry honey, I will wait downstairs and you take as much time as you need."

Ronnie started to panic a little when he glanced at his watch and realized that the limo would be there in a very few minutes.

His first idea was to yell at Cindy and tell her it was time for them to be ready, but then he decided to go upstairs and see what she was doing. He saw his dear wife Cindy in the doorway of their bedroom, holding two pictures in her shaking hands and he could instantly feel her pain. She didn't look up as Ronnie walked over and stood beside her, placing his hand on her shoulder.

"You're a great wife and Mother and I thank God every day for sending you to me. We will never know why God takes one of his children home and leaves the other one in this world. You certainly cannot blame yourself for the car accident that took our son Jimmy, but left Eddy without a scratch. It's been five years and all of us need to move on. We also need to reach out to the son we still have. We are his parents and we can feel the pain he is going through. He has told us many times that it should have been him and not his brother who should have died that day. We certainly are aware that our dear Eddy joined the army, putting himself in harm's way, so that God could take him home and he and Jimmy could be together once again."

Reaching down and taking the pictures from Cindy's trembling hands, Ronnie placed them on the night table. Ronnie held her hand as he helped her up and laughingly said that he would have to take out a second mortgage to pay for this year's anniversary celebration.

"Please, just give me a moment to freshen up and I'll be okay. You go down and tell the driver if he gives you a hard time that he will have to answer to me."

"Wow, can you just believe that it is one o'clock in the morning and that stupid alarm clock will be ringing in a few hours! I don't want to look all frazzled when we get to Church. You know, honey, how some people love to talk."

Two Weeks Later

"Good morning sleepy head. I noticed how you are moving a little slowly today; are you feeling okay? Actually, Ronnie, you are looking a little pale. Do you want to call in sick?"

"Oh no, I'll be okay. It's probably something that I ate yesterday, no need to fuss."

After Ronnie left for work, Cindy had a feeling that something was wrong, so after she cleaned up the kitchen, she decided to go for a little walk and would have a little talk with God.

He would be able to reassure her that everything was going to be alright. She didn't know at that moment, but her life would change that day and never ever be the same again.

Cindy's heart skipped a beat when the phone rang, because she knew in her heart that it would not be good news. She couldn't stop her hand from shaking as she picked up the receiver and said hello.

"Hi Cindy, this is Doug Matthews, Ronnie's boss. We just called an ambulance as we believe he is having a heart attack. They will be taking him to St. Helen's General. I'll be going with him so we will meet there."

Cindy couldn't stop crying and was almost hyperventilating when she walked up the steps and into the emergency room.

As she entered the room, she saw Doug sitting there and she asked how Ronnie was doing and if she would be able to go and see him.

"Actually, Cindy, they took him right into the OR, so we will have to wait until one of the doctors come out to give us an update."

When Cindy's tears stopped, worry set in as a million things crossed through her mind; things like them just making plans to go on a cruise to the Greek Islands and yesterday, they bought Ronnie a box of his favorite cereal and it was the kind she didn't like.

Everything happened so fast and within two days, the love of Cindy's life was gone as God called him home to be with his son Jimmy.

Although both Ronnie's and her family were there for her, Cindy felt totally alone until the day her Eddy arrived home from Iraq. His short stay at home didn't last nearly long enough. He only had a few days at home and then had to return back to his unit.

Cindy never wanted to talk about the army life that Eddy chose as his career. She did know that the pain that her son endured was also her pain. Cindy was determined not to lose her only son, so, she spent every minute with him while he was at home, trying to make up for lost time. She wanted, no needed, to know who her son was and wanted to show him how much she loved him and that they needed each other if they were going to get through this ordeal and move on with their lives.

Eddy shared everything with his Mom, how he felt about Jimmy, choosing the army, and how he shut her and his Dad out so he wouldn't have to deal with reality. He did confess to his Mom, that over the past few months, he found himself thinking a lot about God and how happy he had been as a young boy when Church was a big part of his life. He shared with his Mom how he blamed God for taking his only brother and that he felt it was very unfair.

There had been a change in the departure time of Eddy's flight, so there wasn't much time for long and sad goodbyes.

It was very hard on both of them so the least time they spent dwelling on their loss, the better for both of them. Besides, there would be plenty of time in the future months and years to reflect on the way things are and how they might have been.

Eddy had only been gone a few months when Cindy received a call that he had been injured while on maneuvers. Apparently his truck ran over a roadside bomb. The good news was that no one lost their life, but Eddy was in the hospital undergoing surgery.

After months of rehabilitation, he was sent back to the US for more rehabilitation and then was discharged with honors and was decorated by the Secretary of Defense and once again returned to civilian life.

On November 25th, 2002, Cindy received a bouquet of roses and quickly realized that this was her wedding anniversary. About an hour later, she received a phone call. It was Eddy and he asked her to go to the front door and said he had a surprise for her.

Cindy's heart skipped a beat when she looked outside and saw a white van.

When the side door of the van opened, a ramp appeared and there was her son in a wheelchair. Instantly she started crying as she ran down the driveway to hold her baby.

God works in mysterious ways, his wonders to perform. Life has a way of interfering with our plans and dreams, but God lets us know that it is his will that determines everything.

There is a saying; If you want to make God smile, tell him your plans.

Story Eight

Paid in Full

As I stood in the dimly lit hallway of the "Rest with Us Funeral Home" watching the line of mourners, I, for a brief moment, pictured the person in the all-black casket with pure white linen to be from the Royal Family or a head of state. But it was neither; actually he was "just an ordinary man" although you would be hard pressed to find anyone within a two-hundred-mile radius to agree.

You see, William Boyle (little Billy) to his friends was anything but ordinary. In fact, his four foot ten-inch frame was very deceiving, because to most people who had the honor of having him as a part of their life appeared to them as being well over six feet tall.

Anyway, as I watched the people coming through the door, I couldn't help but notice the variety of characters. Everyone wanted to say their goodbyes to the man that had greatly impacted their lives.

There were old and young, black and white, tall and short and from the very healthy to those in wheelchairs. Even the local politicians waited their turn.

Billy hadn't had a hard life, at least not until his early thirties. You see, his parents were well to do; actually they were one of the richest families in the state.

David W. Boyle, Billy's father, inherited his fortune from his father who didn't come by it honestly. Fortunately, Billy didn't fit in with the influential crowd.

As a matter of fact, if you didn't know him, you would mistake him for a down-and-out street person. This of course drove his parents crazy and so almost after every meal, his father would lecture him and try to convince him that he needed to keep up better appearances.

When Billy's Mother died, the lineup was minimal and sad to say, when his Father left this world, the only ones in attendance were Billy and the Minister and at one point, the cemetery workers stood nearby.

Because of Billy's lifestyle, he was all but left out of the family will. He was left a small trust fund that provided him with a modest income. With the passing of his parents, Billy felt a great sense of freedom that he could now live his life the way he wanted.

The first thing he did was give his life to God.

He had been attending a church for many years, but did not tell his parents, because they didn't need any more reasons to fight with him.

Billy accepted an offer to fill the vacant position at the church to be the caretaker/maintenance person. What he lacked in experience, he made up in enthusiasm.

A humble man, who stayed out of the spotlight, would describe Billy; but if medals were given for all his good deeds, he would have run out of wall space very quickly.

Day after day, year after year, he did what every good Christian should do; He followed in the footsteps of our Lord and Savior.

Although Billy's generosity wasn't limited to the poor, they were usually the recipients of his giving ways. Kids from the poor side of town would get presents for every occasion: birthdays, Christmas, Easter or doing well in sports or school.

Kids weren't the only ones to receive gifts from Billy; anyone in need was on his list. The town had its share of seniors who lived alone and they found it hard to "just get by" but the monthly numinous gifts made life much more bearable for them.

You could call Billy "Robin Hood or Santa Claus," but you would have a hard time giving him any recognition.

He would just deny his role and say that everything comes from God and he would say that as Christians, we need to look after the less fortunate among us.

Billy would also help out the small businessmen who were struggling to keep their doors open.

After about two hours, the line started to thin out, but the funeral home was still full of people wishing to say their goodbyes.

Mr. Cranston, the funeral director, announced that the service was about to begin and he said there was a problem because the room where the service was to take place could only accommodate about a quarter of the mourners.

Everything turned out okay, because Sam Twingel, the owner of the music store, sent some of his staff to pick up enough speakers to allow the service to be heard in about six of the smaller rooms.

"Ladies and gentleman, I guess I forgot to introduce myself. My name is John Gallant and I'm the executor of Billy's last will and testament. When I was helping him make his final arrangements, he hesitated to tell me how much he owed and how much his estate was worth.

Turns out, he owed tens of thousands of dollars in loans from banks, companies and individuals but had not one cent to settle his estate."

John got the shock of his life when he started to receive letters from Billy's creditors and each invoice was marked "Paid in Full."

These are the same words JESUS said as he hung on the cross and looked up to Heaven and uttered the words: "PAID in FULL."

Story Nine

Anger Destroys Everything

The Lord is close to the broken hearted and saves those who are crushed in spirit. (Psalm 34:18)

David felt very uncomfortable as he approached #5 Anger Street. The place looked eerie, like something out of a horror movie. David couldn't help but notice that the front gate was smashed into hundreds of pieces, so he had to watch his step as he walked over a section that had nails protruding out of it.

Once inside the yard, David found himself standing in front of a big red pick-up truck and across the windshield was a sign that read:

```
FOR SALE

By owners wife and son
```

David felt chills going up his spine and the weird feeling didn't leave him as his eyes settled on a wreath hanging on the front door. Taking a deep breath, he rang the doorbell. When no one answered, he knocked a few times and waited. He was about to leave when a woman in a uniform opened the door and asked, "How may I help you Sir?"

"Hello, Ma'am, my name is David McMaster and I'm doing a survey on 'Anger'; I was wondering if I could speak to the homeowner?"

Turning her head, the woman looked into the room behind her and then back at David saying, "You can come in if you wish; the lady of the house is at home today, but she can't speak, so I'll have to answer your questions."

"That's very kind of you, Miss."

"I'm just doing my job, Sir. My name is Caroline; I'm Rose's…sorry, I mean Mrs. Canter's caregiver. Please come in; she's waiting in the living room."

David noticed two things upon entering the room: to his right was a big white leather couch and to his left sitting next to the big picture window was a woman in a wheelchair.

Caroline came into the room and pushed the lady of the house up to the coffee table, directly across from where David had laid his notepad and then sat in a big chair next to her.

Without looking at David, she asked, "How old do you think she is?"

"I'm not good at guessing some one's age but I would say she is probably in her seventies or eighties."

"Would you believe she is only thirty-eight?"

"No way, that's impossible! I don't believe you; please tell me her tragic story!"

"I will, but first, I need to tell you how she aged thirty years in such a short time. It was 'Anger;' not hers, but her husband's. The man had more anger inside of him than this whole town put together. They started dating in high school and then got married when they were in their late twenties. Everyone knew Gordie Canter. The only thing he could do well was body work on cars, so everybody just called him the Tin Man."

"It was obvious he had some major issues and everyone knew it except poor Rose. He had lived with his parents until he and Rose got married and was spoiled rotten, especially by his mother. Whatever he wanted he got or else he made every one's life miserable."

"When Gordie didn't get his own way, he didn't just sulk and stomp his feet; oh no, not the Tin Man! He acted out his 'Anger,' like the time he chopped down his parents' front door and then the telephone pole in front of the house, all because he wanted his own phone in his bedroom and his father refused."

"Gordie's 'Anger' didn't come from what others did to him, but rather from people not allowing him to have everything he wanted. One of his greatest desires in life was to have a son, a little boy he could spoil; but not give him more than he had, so he would always remain the King of the castle."

"Rose didn't want to have children right away, so Gordie was very unhappy. He told her she should have warned him before they got hitched that she didn't want kids."

Her story continued; "One day he said to Rose; "Okay fine; if you can't give me a son, I want a new boat and motor and it has to be the best one on the lake!"

"Gordie, I'm sorry, but we can't afford a new boat; we have too many bills so we can't just buy a boat."

"Are you telling me I can't have a boat?"

"Oh no, Honey! I'm just saying you will have to wait: maybe it will be in our budget next year."

"Fine; if you say no boat then it's no boat."

Rose went to work the next morning hoping that everything would be okay when she got home, but things weren't okay. As a matter of fact, she almost fainted when she walked in the front door and there wasn't one piece of furniture left in the house!

When she approached the back door, she could hear Gordie singing and then she saw him throwing the top of their living room table on a big fire. He greeted her with a smile and called out, "Honey, I thought we could have a BBQ tonight and roast some marshmallows; don't you think that will be a lot of fun?"

The look he gave her sent chills through her body and she could feel her hair stand up on the back of her neck. She should have left him that day but she didn't; sadly, she lived to regret that decision.

"It wasn't long before the Tin Man got his new boat and Rose bought new furniture for the house. He also talked Rose into starting a family and they had a son who they called Tommy. He was Gordie's pride and joy, but when he acted up, he wanted nothing to do with him.

One day, the three of them went shopping. Tommy was about three years old and he saw a train set that he wanted.

When he was told he couldn't have it, he started crying and screaming as loud as he could.

Gordie was very embarrassed and he told Rose to shut him up or else! She picked him up and tried to console him, but that didn't do any good. Gordie looked at her and ordered, "You and your spoiled brat aren't fit to be in a public place; go sit in the car until I'm ready to go home."

Rose and Tommy sat in the scorching heat for about two hours and then Gordie finally came out eating an ice-cream cone and drinking a cold bottle of pop. He walked up to the driver's side of the car and told them to get out. Rose grabbed Tommy and had just enough time to move away from the car as Gordie drove off leaving her on her own.

Here was another opportunity to leave the Tin Man, but once again she went home and thought she would carry on with her life like nothing had happened. As she was walking in the front door with her little Tommy, she heard Gordie yelling from the living room, telling her that he wanted a new red truck.

Rose glared at him, and then threw her arms in the air shouting, "I give up!" Walking into the kitchen she said out loud, "Lord, you're going to have to take him or me, because I can't go on living like this."

She no sooner had the words out of her mouth when she heard a loud noise coming from the living room.

She rushed in and saw Gordie lying on the floor, holding his head and yelling for someone to help him because he couldn't handle the pain. He repeated over and over, "I want my Mommy, I want my Mommy!"

Rose thought she might be able to comfort him so she got down on the floor and put his head on her knees. She told him to relax and everything would be okay. After about ten minutes she stopped rubbing his head because she thought he was sleeping, but he wasn't. Opening his eyes, he declared, "My head doesn't hurt anymore so let's go buy my new red truck."

A week later, Gordie got a call that his new truck was in and he could pick it up whenever he was ready.

"Come on woman; you and the kid need to get ready. You can drive me there and then you can come home on the bus. I sold our piece of junk to that weirdo down the street and I told him to come to the lot and get it, so you better take your garbage out before we go unless you want to bring it home on the bus."

When they arrived at the car lot, Gordie was like a little kid, walking around his new toy, touching it like it was made of pure gold. Rose got out of the car and stood there holding her son Tommy.

"Gordie, what do you want us to do now?"

He gave her his Humphrey Bogart routine and said, "Anything you want Sweetheart, as long as it doesn't involve me or my new red truck."

Rose was too mad to cry and too hurt to say anything else to her husband.

As she exited the bus, Rose looked up the street and all she could see was an enormous big red truck in her driveway. She also noticed there were three men standing on the sidewalk talking to Gordie. When he saw her, he said, "Well I see my lovely wife and my handsome son are home at last!"

When she was close enough, Gordie gave her a slap on the behind and laughed out loud saying, "Get in the house woman and fix my supper, while I talk to these men!"

From inside, Rose walked over to the front window and could see that Gordie was giving the men instructions to build him a new fence.

After the men left, Gordie came inside and told her that they would have the fence and gate finished by the end of the week. He wasn't talking to anyone in particular, just saying out loud what was going to happen.

Sure enough, the fence was up in a few days. After he inspected it thoroughly, he told the man to go to the house and his wife would pay him.

"You'll have to take a check, because I don't have enough cash on me."

Rose asked, "How much will it be, Sir?"

"When we put on another coat of paint it will be $499.95 plus tax."

Rose looked at him and exclaimed, "That's a lot of money for twenty feet of fence and a gate!"

The man explained, "It would have been a lot less, but your husband wanted special wood and a rush job."

"Here you go," Rose said, as she handed the check to the worker. When she looked out the big picture window, she could see Gordie on his hands and knees, obviously in a lot of pain.

Calling out, "Excuse me," she ran past the contractor and out the door to help her man. One of the workers asked her if she needed any help.

Without looking up she said, "No thank you, I'll be okay." With a concerned look on her face, she asked Gordie if he wanted her to call the doctor.

"No, it's just one of my stupid headaches; just help me to get into the house."

Rose might have been small but she managed to get him into the house. As she helped him into one of the big chairs in the living room she said, "Honey you've been suffering from terrible headaches lately; maybe you need some medicine to control the pain."

"Listen to me woman; do you think I'm stupid or what? I know you just want to get me doped up with pills and then sign me into a loony bin, so you and your boyfriend can ride all over town in my new red truck!"

"Don't talk like that, Gordie! I love you and I don't want any other man in my life."

"Well, I'm not taking any chances; I'm putting a lock on the gate just in case!"

Over the next few weeks, the headaches became a lot worse and were happening more frequently.

Black Saturday

There was nothing unusual about the start of the day. Rose was doing her house cleaning and Gordie was out in the garage, hammering away on an old car.

He needed some tools from the basement but didn't want to leave Tommy alone; then he saw that the gate was closed and his little boy was playing in the sand box, so he decided to make a run for it.

He was gone a lot longer than he expected and when he walked out on to the deck, he dropped the tools and started screaming, "Get away from my truck, you little monster!"

Tommy thought his daddy was just having fun with him so he ran around to the other side of the truck and continued hitting it with the hammer. He kept saying over and over, "Look at me Daddy; I'm fixing your truck!"

Gordie was getting one of his headaches as he chased little Tommy around the truck. Finally, he decided to just stop and wait and when he did, Tommy ran right into his arms.

Grabbing the hammer from his little hand, Gordie raised it over his head and was mad enough to hit his son!

When he heard Rose pounding on the big picture window, he lowered it and pushed his son to the ground, giving his wife a look that said, "It's your entire fault!"

Before Gordie could walk away he felt Tommy grab hold of his leg and through his tears he cried, "Why are you mad at me Daddy?"

With one shake of his leg he made his crying boy fall back and as he hit his head on the hammer he lay there in silence.

Stepping over his son's body, his head filled with rage, Gordie grabbed his keys; he took one last look at all the dents in his beautiful red truck and climbed into the driver's seat.

After pounding on the steering wheel four or five times he started the engine, and without a backward glance, he grabbed the truck door and slammed it shut with all his strength.

In a blind rage, Gordie wasn't aware of his surroundings; he just wanted to get away, but to where, he didn't know.

Hearing the truck door slam shut with a huge bang it startled Rose and she ran to the window. She was just in time to see the big black tires spraying dirt and gravel, while at the same time the front end of the big red monster made contact with the white picket fence.

The truck was now out of control and swerving from side to side; it seemed to have a mind of its own.

With one quick movement, the three-thousand-pound red pile of steel went into a spin. It took only a split second for the rear end to come around and strike Mr. Goodman as he walked across the road.

Back at the house, Rose stood in shock and disbelief as she looked down at her son laying still, "Just the way he looked when she would go into his room at night to check on him;" but her motherly instincts brought her back to reality and she let out a scream as she cried for help.

In a matter of seconds she was out the front door and racing across the lawn. Falling on her knees, she cuddled her precious little boy. He wasn't moving, but she could hear his heart beating.

Looking up at the sky through her tears, she pleaded, "God, please don't take my son; he's all I have left in the world!"

Unaware of what just happened, Gordie gained control of the truck and once again stepped on the gas pedal, making the tires squeal.

Mike Anderson, a neighbor, stood on his lawn and watched in horror as the unbelievable scene unfolded.

Without concern for his own safety, Mike stepped onto the road and started waving his hands and then braced himself for the impact.

It wasn't until later that another neighbor told him, "You looked just like David when he stood his ground in front of Goliath."

The truck stopped just a few feet from his now trembling body. Gordie was livid and started yelling at his neighbor, but stopped when Mike pointed back and shouted, "Look what you've done! Not even God will forgive you for this."

As Mike was running back to see if he could be of help, he could hear the ambulance in the distance and least a dozen people were now offering advice as they waited for help to arrive.

Gordie seemed to be in shock as he passed Mr. Goodman's covered body; he then let out a scream as he looked at Rose holding their little boy. As he ran toward them he kept saying over and over, "I killed my son, I killed my son."

Rose didn't look up at him; as far as she was concerned he was out of their lives forever.

A woman standing on the sidewalk hollered out, "Is there a doctor or nurse on our street?" but before anyone could answer her, the ambulance arrived.

After examining Tommy, one of the medics proclaimed, "The little fellow is breathing, but we need to get him to the hospital right away."

They had trouble getting the stretcher into the truck because Rose was hanging on with both hands and wouldn't let go; she kept repeating, "God please take me and let my son live!"

After ten long hours of surgery, one of the doctors came in to the waiting room and said; I'm sorry Mrs. Canter; we were able to save your son's life, but he's in a coma and there may be some brain damage; the way the flying rocks hit his face, he will most likely have permanent facial scars. He's in God's hands now."

Rose fell to her knees and as she lifted her head towards Heaven, she cried out loud, "God, why is this happening to us? He's only a baby and now he has to go through life scarred because of someone else? Why didn't you just take me and let my son grow up to be a man and have a family of his own; it's just not fair!"

The doctor lifted her up and said, "Don't be mad at God; He's not responsible for what happened to your little boy."

Before he left the room, the doctor advised Rose that he would instruct the nurse to give her something to help her cope.

It was a few days before Rose was able to go home and take a much needed bath and get some clean clothes.

When she arrived at the house, she knew something was wrong. The front door was wide open and the house was in darkness. As she walked in the door, she turned on the hall light, and although the kitchen light wasn't on, she noticed a light coming from the basement. The basement door was wide open so she started to walk down the stairs, hollering out, "Gordie are you down there?"

She waited a few seconds and when she didn't get a reply, she continued down. As she reached the last step she had to grip the handrail as her eyes fixed on the horrific scene of her husband's lifeless body hanging from one of the wooden rafters. Rose was totally overwhelmed and her mind quickly recalled another familiar scenario from the Bible, when Judas betrayed Jesus and paid the ultimate price by allowing Satan to be his executioner.

Spellbound by Caroline's story, David had to wipe away the tears from his eyes as he questioned, "Whatever happened to Tommy?"

She smiled and asked, "Would you like to meet him?"

"Yes, please!"

Getting up quickly, she stood in the hallway and hollered out, "Tommy, there's someone here who wants to meet you!"

David was totally unprepared as he watched a smiling young boy wheel himself into the room. From a distance he looked fine and it wasn't until he came closer that David could see the deep scars on his face and a small metal plate on the side of his little bald head.

David was speechless and Tommy could see that he wasn't going to say anything, so he just smiled and said, "Hi! My name is Tommy; it's nice to meet you, Sir."

As David knelt down, he felt very uncomfortable but Tommy put him at ease asking, "Did you know my Daddy? Mommy said he wasn't happy with us, so God took him to Heaven. Someday, I'm going to go see him and maybe I'll drive there in his big red truck!"

David enjoyed visiting with Tommy and it was a long time before he could say, "I have to go."

As he was leaving, he remembered the baby he and Emily lost and how he missed the chance to be a father.

Of all the people and stories David had encountered on his trip, none was more moving than the one he heard at #6 Anger Street. There was no need for words as he waved to Tommy and walked out the front door. He tried not to look back as he walked down the winding walkway and stepped over the broken pieces of the wooden fence.

David's emotions got the best of him and he turned around and looked at the house and then at the red truck one more time; then as he shook his head, he could see the Bible opened to (Mathew 16:26)

"What good will it be for someone to gain the whole world, yet forfeit their soul? Or what can anyone give in exchange for their soul?"

The heart wrenching story at # 6 Anger Street made David's blood run cold; it was almost more than he could handle so he needed "The Golden Bench" now more than ever and God didn't disappoint him. There, just a few feet away was "The Golden Bench" and as he approached, he was a little surprised when the envelope floated into his hands; with a sigh of relief he sat down in the "Place of Peace."

David removed the paper from the envelope and started to read:

I the Lord have forgiven you for the times you've failed to give me first place in your life. So open your heart and I will walk with you every step of the way. I will teach you how to tune out the noises and distractions of the world, so that you can tune in to my voice and aim your prayers with precision toward Heaven. I want to lead you into a deeper and more rewarding relationship with me!

Nothing can give you peace or change your life more than hearing and trusting in my word. I the Lord will speak words of wisdom and comfort to you and all you have to do is sit quietly in my presence.

I will also refresh you, and give you rest, so that you may experience my presence, power, and peace.

Story Ten

Enter Shakespeare

David was not surprised when the "Man in White" stood before him and spoke these words into his head: "2 Thessalonians says; 'there will be a shout of command, the archangel's voice, the sound of God's trumpet, and the Lord himself will come down from heaven.

Those who have died believing in Christ will rise to life first; then we who are living at the time will be gathered up alone with them to meet the Lord in the air. And so we will always be with the Lord. So then, encourage one another with these words.'"

Bob elaborated, "There's an old movie theatre and it shows the same picture over and over again. I think it's a (Revised) version of Romeo and Juliet but I've never stopped long enough to see it all the way through. Apparently it's got a good message and it's helped a lot of people but I'm not into that movie stuff. If it had some ladies running around half dressed, I might check it out."

They were totally exhausted by the time they got to the exit, because it was a lot further than they had expected.

So after putting down their burdens, Bob and David just stood there looking at the marquee on the side of the old dilapidated movie house.

"Look," Bob pointed out. "That's the movie I told you would be playing. I think it's about two kids who fall in love. The girl's parents don't like her choice so I think they commit suicide, but I don't know for sure."

After a few minutes David suggested, "Let's go watch it; if we don't enjoy it, we can always go to sleep for a few hours."

"Sure, you talked me into it. I can always use a little sleep."

"What about our burdens; do you think they'll be okay?"

Bob replied, "Nobody would ever steal someone's burdens, why would they? Actually the worst thing about burdens is that you can't sell, give, or donate them to anyone else. They're yours until you deal with them; no matter how long it takes."

"Boy, this place sure is an oldie," David remarked as he walked up to the lady in the cashier's booth. "I'll have two tickets please;" but when he didn't receive a reply he asked again putting his mouth closer to the little round metal piece in the center of the window.

He jumped back when he realized that what he thought was a woman was actually a robot. Its head came off its shoulders and smashed into the window. Startled, David jumped back and watched as the head recoiled back on the robot's shoulders. With flashing red eyes it spoke, "I heard you the first time; I have perfect hearing you know. Just go in, you don't need tickets. It's easy to see you don't have any money and I've seen your friend around here before; I know for a fact that he doesn't have a penny to his name."

Once inside the room David commented, "I think the show is about to start so let's find a seat."

Although it was dark, David's eyes adjusted quickly and he turned to Bob saying, "Something weird is going on here.

From the outside the building looks like it could hold a few hundred people, but now that we're inside I can see that it's the smallest theater in the world. It only has six seats and four of them are taken. Come on let's grab those two empty ones before someone else gets them."

After looking around the small room for a few minutes David elbowed Bob, reiterating, "There's something very odd about this place!"

His eyes settled on the four people behind him. Clearly, they didn't look like real people, more like mannequins.

There was a middle aged couple and an older woman with a young teenage girl sitting next to her.

The movie was on pause and only started when David and Bob were seated and looking at the screen. Within ten minutes David jabbed Bob in the ribs and ordered, "Watch this!"

When he turned his head away, the movie stopped and when he looked back it started again. Bob suggested, "Let me try it." He turned away really fast and then back again and the same thing happened.

"We can forget about sleeping," David said. "Because if one of us closes our eyes the movie will stop and we won't miss a thing. So I guess we'll just have to watch it to the end."

When the boys finely settled down and watched the screen they saw a graveyard with a Preacher and about a dozen people staring at a headstone that read…

Richard Copeland
1979-1996
In Loving memory
From
Juliet, to her Romeo

As the camera panned through the crowd, David saw four people who looked familiar, very familiar; as a matter of fact, they were sitting in the seats directly behind him.

"Hey Bob, the cast of this movie are in the building; maybe we can get their autographs after the show!"

The screen changed and there was a young couple kissing and holding each other close. In the next scene, they were walking in a wooded area and when they reached a fork in the road, they kissed again. The boy just stood there shaking his head as he watched the young girl disappear behind some trees.

The next scene was of a set of iron gates with a sign that read…

The Estate of

Willard and Maureen

Vanderhoff

The scene changes again and we see the same young girl walking into her house. Well, maybe we should say mansion, because this was definitely not your ordinary poor row house.

The two homes did have something in common; whether you're rich or poor you have problems. It's just easier for the rich to cover them up.

"Brenda, where have you been? I thought I told you to come home right after school!"

Brenda didn't say a word; she just gave her Mother a look and then started up the big wooden staircase.

"Where are you going young lady? I'm talking to you! How dare you; don't you ever turn your back to me!" But when she made a grab for her daughter she tripped and spilled some of her drink.

With an arrogant tone in her voice, Brenda looked at her mother and said, "Don't worry about the carpet Mommy dearest; there's enough booze in it to keep you and Daddy drunk for a whole year."

"Don't use that tone of voice with me; I'm your Mother and you will show me some respect!"

Brenda shouted back as she reached the top of the stairs, "You don't have any respect for yourself Mother, so why should I have any for you?"

Not much was said that night at dinner, but the air was heavy and Brenda knew that before the meal was finished, there would be a heated argument.

Every night, before, during or after dinner, the same topic was discussed. Her father would start with, "Your mother told me that you were late coming home again today and that you talked back to her. I've told you many times I will not tolerate that kind of behavior in my house. Now that I have your attention, I hope you are not still seeing that kid Tricky or Spiky or whatever his name is. He's not the kind of guy that you should be hanging around because he won't amount to anything; those people never do."

Brenda spoke up, "For the hundredth time Daddy, his name is Rickey, and he is going to be a 'somebody' someday. He's the one that I want to spend the rest of my life with!"

Her Father stood up and shouted, "If you disobey me again, I will put you back in private school; at least you'll be with your own kind. We should have never agreed to let you go to a public school; they're filled with social rejects and only teach rebellion. The garbage that they speak and the weird music they play is the reason why this world is falling apart."

"I'm sure the drinking and prescription drugs you and Mom use is a wonderful example to pass along to us, the next generation!"

Her Father stared at her and for the first time in her life, she saw him at a loss for words. He just sat down and continued eating. Brenda's mom tried to stand up, but even holding onto the table and the back of the chair, she could barely get to her feet. Slurring her words she said, "Willard is that all you are going to say to your daughter?"

"You should talk Mother, the phony way you and Daddy live; always putting on airs, thinking you're better than everyone else! You're such a great example for me to live by. Maybe someone should make a movie or TV show so the whole world can see how a perfect family lives!" She then turned to walk away but stopped and with a little more contempt in her voice remarked, "If I'm going to turn out like you two, I'd rather die now!"

The next day Brenda's heart skipped a beat as she stood near a little bridge and watched her Ricky walking towards her. They hugged and he gave her a little kiss on the cheek. "I can see that you and your parents had another battle," he pointed to her red eyes.

"It doesn't matter," Brenda said, giving him another squeeze. "Let's not spoil our day talking about them."

Excitedly, Brenda continued, "I love the story of 'Romeo and Juliet'; do you think you will get to play the part of Romeo?"

Ricky didn't answer her, he just hung his head. As they started walking toward their school, Brenda gave her quiet shy man a big hug saying, "I'm so proud of you!"

They didn't talk for a long time as they walked hand in hand. Brenda was first to break the silence and in almost a whisper she said, "I wish I was Juliet and then we could die in each other's arms. Wouldn't that be great?"

"Rickey just looked at her wondering, "Would she really die to prove her undying love for me?" The two love birds were just coming out of the wooded area when they spotted Ricky's arch enemy big, Johnny Summerville. Looking down at the two of them Johnny remarked, "Well, well, what do we have here?"

Ricky dropped Brenda's hand and with a little push put her behind him for protection. Johnny stood right in front of the couple and because he was over six foot tall he easily dwarfed them.

Ricky tried to get in Johnny's face, but they were standing so close that all he could see was the big guy's chest. He then tried to step back but Johnny just talked over him and commented to Brenda, "Why don't you get rid of this loser and be my girl again? I'm sure you miss being with a real man."

Ricky moved to his right to try and go around the massive body blocking his path. He only moved about two feet when he felt a big hand around his throat and then he felt his feet leaving the ground. He tried with all his strength to break the hold on his neck, but with each passing minute Ricky could feel his body going limp.

Brenda was screaming out loud, "Please help us, he's going to kill Ricky!!"

Out of nowhere came the very familiar face of Mr. Munford, the gym instructor. Reaching up he quickly grabbed Big Johnny under the right arm squeezing with all his strength. This caused the big guy to scream out loud and he reluctantly released his hold on Ricky's throat.

When Johnny turned and saw that it was Mr. Munford attacking him, he stopped swearing and fell to his knees. He didn't stay down for long and when he got to his feet he muttered something under his breath, and then headed for the school without looking back.

Looking at Mr. Munford Brenda questioned, "How did you make Johnny release Rickey so quickly? All I could see was your hand going under his arm."

"As you can see I'm not much bigger than Ricky so I had to learn to defend myself, or I would have to go through life taking beatings from the big 'Johnny's' of this world. So my five years in the Marines and a black belt in Karate came in handy. Oh! One more thing; always remember that life is about choices so always try to make the right ones!"

Brenda pondered, "So much for the mild mannered Gym teacher!"

Ricky didn't comment; he just lowered his head and walked away. He was embarrassed once again in front of his girlfriend. He didn't know it at the time, but Brenda loved him more than life and when they were together, he didn't need to prove he was a man.

Thanking Mr. Munford, Brenda hurried off to catch up to Ricky. By the time she reached the road in front of the school, he was already going through the big double doors.

The rest of the day didn't go well for Ricky. The story of how Mr. Munford had to rescue him from big bad Johnny went around the school faster than a speeding bullet. Brenda waited at the main door of the gym until after five o'clock. The drama class students were filling into the room and the auditions were starting.

After some minor roles were filled, the call went out for the students who were trying out for the two main characters, Romeo and Juliet. Even Mr. Jackman, the director, seemed to be stalling a little bit hoping to see Ricky walk through the doors.

When he couldn't wait any longer, he asked the ladies to come forward. It took only about fifteen minutes to select Mary Stinebrack, a beautiful grade eleven student to play Juliet. Her mother and father were well known in the entertainment industry.

The director took one last look around the room, and then he gave a signal for the boys wanting to play Romeo to come on the stage. It took longer to choose Romeo but finally Stan Johnston, a shy but very good looking boy was chosen. After thanking everyone, the director announced that rehearsals would start next Monday.

Brenda walked home very slowly hoping that Ricky would come up behind her or jump out from behind a tree but that didn't happen. As soon as she got into the house she called Ricky but he wasn't at home. She did get to talk to his grandmother. "Hello, Mrs. Manning this is Brenda, a friend of Ricky's. Do you know when he'll be home? He was at school today but he left early."

With a shaky voice she replied, "No I haven't seen him since this morning. What did you say your name was?"

"Brenda; please have Ricky call me as soon as he comes in."

The next day was Friday and Ricky didn't show up for his first class. Brenda was getting really worried so she called his grandmother again.

Mrs. Manning admitted, "I've been worried too since he didn't come home last night; that's not like Ricky to stay out all night and not call me."

She told Brenda that she didn't know where he was but she was praying nothing bad had happened to him. "I'm just his Grandmother and I love him dearly, but we can't communicate. He's been through a lot and I'm sure he feels deserted.

His father is in jail and his mother left him on my doorstep with nothing but a small suitcase and a few dollars in his pocket. Even before he came to live with me, I was finding it hard to get by with my small pension, but Ricky tried to help out by working part time. Even that money is gone since some man named Mr. Vanderhoff spoke to his boss."

A few days later Brenda got a call from Rickey's grandmother, telling her she had just seen Rickey. "He only stayed a few minutes, just long enough to tell me he was staying with some friends and not to worry. I told him you had called and that you needed to see him. He said to tell you that you're better off without him, and that you need to find someone from your own world to love. He also said that your father was right; he's just a loser from the wrong side of the tracks."

Through her tears Brenda asked, "Did he say where he was staying?"

"No, but he did make it very clear that he didn't want to see you anymore. I'm sorry my dear, but that's life."

Brenda let the phone drop out of her hand and fell back into a big chair and couldn't stop crying.

An hour later her mother staggered by the living room door and watched her sobbing and asked, "What's wrong with you; are you sick or what?"

Brenda didn't reply; she just gave her mother a dirty look and made a motion with her hand telling her to go away.

"Okay, if that's the way you feel I'll leave."

Giving Brenda a dirty look she stumbled and spilled the last of her drink on her already messy dress. "Now look what you've done!" as she made a loud burp and walked away.

When Brenda didn't come down for dinner, her father went up to check on her. He went to her room and knocked a few times, but when she didn't answer he went back downstairs.

Sitting at the dinner table, Willard looked at his half-asleep wife and questioned, "Did you see Brenda go out or were you sleeping most of the day?"

"If I had someone to talk to I wouldn't have to get drunk or stoned and maybe I could stay awake. All I can remember was her sitting in a chair crying and when I asked her why, she just dismissed me with a flick of her hand."

"Oh well, she'll come home when she hungry. I'm not going to worry about her, let's just eat dinner. I've got some work to do tonight so it will be quiet around here for a change."

Brenda had her mother's car, but she knew it wouldn't be missed, because it was always in the garage. Her mother had lost her license last year for a DUI and her dad always parked in the driveway. He wouldn't notice that his wife's car was gone.

Driving around crying and confused, Brenda didn't know where to go or who to call. She knew Ricky didn't have very many friends but there was one guy at school named "Ragman" that he sometimes talked to. The guy was known for selling drugs, but as far as she knew, Ricky didn't do drugs or drink.

Brenda remembered a place in town called "Crazy Eddie's" where a lot of the kids from her school hung out. People said it wasn't a nice place, but because she had never been inside she really didn't know how bad it was.

Sitting outside the bar for a long time, Brenda tried to get enough nerve to go in. She knew the place was hopping because she could hear the loud music and could see a stream of kids coming and going. After thinking about Ricky for a while, she dried her eyes and got into the long lineup. She couldn't help but hear a girl in the line say to her friend, "Will you look at who's here? I guess we'll have to find somewhere else to hang out now that the rich people are starting to frequent the place. I'm sure the management will be putting the prices up so high that we poor folk will have to go somewhere else to drink!"

Brenda just ignored her and besides, no one was listening to the loud mouth anyway. The line moved quickly and before Brenda knew it, she was inside the cattle barn.

Although the place was packed solid, Brenda recognized a lot of the kids, but she didn't know any of their names.

Brenda was very good looking and because she wore very expensive clothes, she stood out from the rest of the crowd.

A few guys gave her the once-over but soon realized she was out of their league. One guy was standing a few feet away and kept staring at her like he knew her, but was surprised to see her in a place like this.

Walking over and standing beside her, he said, "Hi I'm Sean. You probably don't remember me but I'm a friend of your ex-boyfriend, Johnny Summerville."

Without looking at him Brenda replied, "That's nice."

He questioned, "So how come you're in a place like this? It's definitely not your average Country Club! I know you're not here to score some drugs, because all you rich people have to do is place an order and it's delivered to your front door, or should I say, back door."

Giving him a dirty look she said; "It must be a tough life if the only friend you have is Johnny Summerville. By the way, the only reason I'm here is to find a friend who is very important to me. Do you know a guy that hangs out here sometimes, called Ragman?"

"Maybe I do; is he a friend of your friend?"

Not waiting for an answer Sean continued, "What was your friend's name again?"

"His name is Ricky, Ricky Copeland."

"You don't mean Ricky Copeland the loser. I heard he's a little fairy, if you know what I mean; he likes boys not girls!"

Sean was starting to get to her, so in a very loud voice she blurted out, "You don't know what you're talking about. I'll tell you something squirt; Ricky's my boyfriend and he's more of a man than you and Johnny Summerville will ever be. So just tell me if you know the 'Ragman' or not! If you don't, then just go away and leave me alone."

"Okay! I know him, he'll be here soon and I'll introduce you, but you'll have to get in line, because the minute he walks through that door there will be people all over him. He sells the stuff dreams are made of and tonight he'll be make a lot of people very, very happy. I think he should be called the 'Candy Man' not the 'Ragman'."

Standing by the door Brenda waited for the only person who might know where she can find her Ricky. It wasn't long before someone yelled out, "The Ragman's here, so let's all pool our money and buy lots of that good stuff and then we can party all night long!"

Brenda could see the young people's smiling faces as they formed a big line in front of the most popular guy in the room.

Waiting patiently till the line got smaller, Brenda finally got her first look at the "Ragman." But before she could get to him someone came over and whispered something in his ear and he bolted towards the exit door. Brenda was right behind calling, "Wait, I need to talk to you! Please, it's about Ricky Copeland, I'm his girlfriend."

The "Ragman" stopped when he got to the end of the alleyway and yelled back at her, "Look lady, I just give them what they want and if they don't get it from me, they'll get it from someone else."

Brenda caught up to him saying, "Please just tell me where Ricky is so I can help him."

"I think he's down on Jarvis Street; there's a flop house near the Belmont Hotel."

Before he could finish what he was saying he was surrounded by five big burly policemen. One big officer came up beside them and commented, "Well, well what do we have here, Bonnie and Clyde?"

Brenda looked at the officer pointedly; "I'm not with him. I was just asking him if he had seen my friend."

"Sure you were; and he can give you and your friend a magic carpet rides to a land where you'll live happily ever after." The officer then made a motion to one of the other policeman to take them both away.

One of the officers from 52 Division called Brenda's father and advised, "We're holding your daughter on charges of selling drugs."

In a very harsh voice Mr. Vanderhoff hollered into the phone, "I'll be right there with my lawyer and you better be treating my daughter like she is one of your own kids, do you hear me?"

After hitting speed dial, Brenda's father put the phone on speaker so he could grab his coat and hat while he waited for someone to answer.

"Hello, this is the office of Richard M. Clark, Barrister; how may I help?"

"This is Willard Vanderhoff; tell Richard to meet me at 52 Division right away!"

Walking into 52 Division, Mr. Vanderhoff yelled out, "I want to see my daughter now!"

The on duty Sergeant came out from behind his desk saying, "Sir, please calm down and I'll try to help you."

"I won't sit down and I demand that you bring my daughter out here immediately!"

"What's your daughter's name, Sir?"

In a very loud voice he replied, "Its Brenda Vanderhoff," as he tried to push the officer out of his way.

"Please Sir, just sit down and relax."

"Don't tell me to relax; I'm Brenda's father and you're treating her like a common criminal. I want to speak to Chief Miller right now!"

"I'm sorry Sir, but Chief Miller is not available. He works out of head office and besides, he doesn't work nights; if you'll just take a seat I'll try to help you."

Willard Vanderhoff finally sat down but he was very agitated. He kept asking questions but no one was listening to him. The ringing of his phone startled him, but he calmed down when he heard his wife's voice.

"What's going on Willard and when are you bringing our daughter home?"

"I'm trying to get her out of here, but these people aren't cooperating. Maureen, I have to go, Richard just walked in. Yes, I'll call you later; I'm sure everything is going to be okay."

Hi Willard, sorry about the tuxedo, but I was at a dinner party when I received your message. So what's the problem my friend?"

"Maureen and I were just sitting at home when we got a call from the police saying they arrested Brenda for drugs. Please just get my daughter out of here!"

Richard went over to the sergeant and introduced himself. "I'm Brenda Vanderhoff's lawyer; may I see her?"

"She's in a holding cell and you can't see her until she's been booked and questioned by one of our drug squad officers."

"Listen Sergeant, I don't want to go over your head but if I have to I will. This is Mr. Willard Vanderhoff's daughter; he's a very prominent citizen with very important friends."

"I'm sure he is, but we have to follow rules and the rules apply to everyone, rich or poor."

Richard stepped back and taking out his phone he dialed Chief Miller. "Sorry to bother you at home, Ralph, but we have a situation down here at 52Division. I'm with Bill Vanderhoff and they have his daughter in custody and they won't let me see her. Okay, thanks Ralph."

Turning to the Sergeant he told him, "Your boss wants to talk to you."

"Yes Sir, I understand completely."

The very apologetic Sergeant handed the phone back to Richard and told him, "I'll have Miss Vanderhoff brought up to the first interview room on the left."

Mr. Vanderhoff was pacing the floor when he saw an officer bringing Brenda down the hall in handcuffs. In a loud voice he ordered, "Get those handcuffs off my daughter!"

Richard stepped in front of him and said to the officer, "Are those really necessary?"

"Yes" was the reply; "its protocol."

The Sergeant came from behind his desk and said, "It's okay officer; just remove the handcuffs and go back down stairs."

He then pointed to one of the rooms saying, "You guys can talk in there while I get the release papers."

Richard nodded to Willard; "You go in with Brenda and I'll look after the paperwork."

"What's going on Brenda, were you selling drugs?"

"Absolutely not; why would you even ask?"

"Then tell me why you were hanging around with those people?"

"I was looking for Ricky; you know the loser that you had fired from his part time job?"

"Brenda you're my whole life and I was only trying to protect you. I don't know why you can't see that."

"Oh no Dad; you're not trying to protect me, you're only worried about your reputation, Mr. big businessman. You only care about your rich country club friends and those faceless boardroom puppets that you call staff. You and Mom may be able to fool the public, but I know the real rich hypocrites that live in our mansion at 63227 Balmoral Drive. I'm telling you right know Dad; if anything happens to Ricky and I find out that it was your fault, I'll never forgive you!"

Standing in the doorway, Richard said, "Sorry to interrupt you Willard, but I've completed all the paper work, so you can take Brenda home now."

"Thanks for all your help Richard."

"No problem, you'll get my bill in the morning."

As they drove home, there was little to no conversation between Brenda and her father. When they entered the house, Brenda's mom tried to give her a hug, but she walked right by her and ran upstairs. "Willard, what's going on?"

"I don't know where we went wrong, but I feel like we're losing our daughter. We gave her everything and now this is how she is treating us. She has a choice to make; it's either him or us."

The next morning Brenda wasted no time contacting Ricky's grandmother. "Hi, Mrs. Manning; this is Brenda, have you heard from Ricky?"

"No dear, but I've been praying day and night. I'm so worried that something bad will happen to him. I've even asked God to protect him and bring him home safe and sound." Through her tears Brenda said, "I promise you that I will find him and bring him home."

To say Brenda was scared was an understatement. The thought of going into an old dilapidated building on Jarvis Street to face her worst nightmares sent a chill down her spine.

Another problem she needed to solve was her wardrobe, because she would stand out like a sore thumb wearing anything from her closet.

She remembered some old clothes in the basement that she wore for Halloween one year and along with her dad's old weather-beaten baseball hat, she was sure she would fit right in.

Brenda tried not to make eye contact with the poor souls she passed on Jarvis street. She felt relieved when she saw an old rusty sign that read The Belmont Hotel. She jumped when she heard a gruff voice question, "Hey, ya got any change or a cigarette?"

Trying to sound tough Brenda shouted, "No I ain't got anything; do I look rich to you?"

When Brenda reached the corner, she stood in front of the building not knowing what to do next. She could see an old man leaning against a door that was hanging by one hinge. "Who are you looking for, Lady?"

Brenda looked him over and thought what the heck; 'I need help and this guy is as good as anyone.' Giving him a little smile she asked, "I guess I stand out like a sore thumb?"

"Oh no, not really; lots of people come to this part of town looking for one thing or another. When I looked at you, I knew you needed help. Do you want to buy some stuff?"

"Oh no, I'm just looking for a friend. I think he's got himself into a mess that he can't get out of on his own."

"You got a picture of your friend?"

"Yes I do," she replied as she handed him a small snapshot of her and Ricky.

"This might be your lucky day lady; come with me."

Brenda hesitated for a moment and then thought to herself, 'if I don't go now, I may never see Ricky again.'

"Well, what'll it be Lady? Do you want me to take you to him or not? I might be down and out but I'm not a bad person, so it's up to you."

"Okay Sir, lead the way."

The old man took a few steps and without turning around he warned, "This ain't the Ritz; you might not like what you see, but don't judge them. They didn't ask for this kind of life, they just made the wrong choices and now they are paying for it."

Brenda couldn't believe her eyes. She knew homeless people had a hard life, but she wasn't prepared for what she was seeing. Stepping over a guy with a needle hanging out of his arm, Brenda made it to the first step, but then cringed and almost lost her balance as her shoe made contact with human excrement.

However, the trouble she was having with all the obstacles was nothing compared to the stench!

Brenda felt herself getting sicker by the minute as the fresh air diminished the deeper she went into the building.

The old man stopped and pointed to a room at the end of the dark hallway and then looked at her and smiled saying, "How about a few dollars for my troubles?"

"Sure," Brenda replied as she handed him a ten dollar bill. Grabbing the money and moving away quickly, Brenda heard him say "Thanks Lady, I hope you're not too late."

Brenda just stood there trying to understand what the old man meant by his remark. Then she thought, 'I've come this far; I can't turn around now.'

As she slowly opened the door and looked inside, she could discern everything in the room but there was no sign of life.

As her eyes adjusted even more she could make out two people; one was sitting on a box and the other was on the floor with their back against the wall. "Ricky, is that you?"

"Who wants to know?"

"It's me Ricky; I'm so glad I found you! Please get up and come home with me. You know you don't belong here."

"No, you're the one who shouldn't be here. Why don't you go back to your world and ask your rich daddy to donate a few bucks to make this flop house into a Social Club?"

"Please Ricky, stop saying those things and come with me. We need to get out of here now!"

Ricky just laughed out loud, sarcastically replying, "I'll go with you to your house if I can bring all my buddies."

Ricky, it's not my fault that I was born into a rich family; I don't like it any more than you do. Please believe me; I'd give up everything to spend the rest of my life with you!"

Her heart skipped a beat when she saw him coming towards her. "Do you really mean it; you would give up everything for me?"

"Yes Ricky, trust me; I love you that much!"

"Okay we'll get out of here; but if you're lying to me, I'll come back here and you'll never see me again."

Ricky's grandmother started crying and thanking God for bringing him home safely to her.

After hugging her for a few minutes she insisted, "You go and get cleaned up while I fix something to eat."

"Oh I can't stay Mrs. Manning, I have some things to take care of, but I'll be back later."

After kissing Ricky on the cheek and giving him a big hug, Brenda said, "I promise you my love, I'll be back in a few hours."

When Brenda entered her house, she saw four suitcases in the hallway and could hear her parents talking in the living room. "What's going on; are you guys going on a trip?"

Her mother stood up and walked toward her smiling, "We're all going on a nice long vacation. I've packed a bag for you honey and if I've forgotten anything, we can just buy it later."

Brenda's father was on the phone and when he finished, he turned to the girls saying, "All set, the limo will be here in twenty minutes."

Brenda started to back out of the room insisting, "I'm not going anywhere!"

"Oh yes you are!" her father demanded. "You're only seventeen and you'll do as I say.

You'll have to wait till next year to ruin your life, but for now, this family will live by my rules."

Crying uncontrollably, Brenda ran upstairs to her room and threw herself on the bed. She didn't lay there for very long because she realized that she only had a few minutes to reach Ricky and try to explain why she had to break her promise to him.

Grabbing the phone by her bed she dialed Ricky's number. She panicked when she heard Mrs. Manning's voice.

"Hi Brenda, are you coming over?"

"No, not right now, can I speak to Ricky please?"

"He's still in the shower and I'm sure he'll be in there for a while."

"Listen to me; I need you to tell him that something has come up and I have to go away for a little while, but when I come back, we'll be together forever."

Three days later

"Hi Mrs. Manning, this is Brenda; Can I speak to Ricky?"

"I'm sorry he's not here. He left just after you called the other day and I haven't seen or heard from him since.

I did tell him you would call him when you got back, but he muttered something about a promise and that you let him down, just like everyone else. I remember him saying something about a revised version of Romeo and Juliet, where only Romeo dies."

"Why don't you come and visit me, my Dear, and together we can pray and ask God to bring our Ricky home safely?"

Brenda couldn't speak. She just let the phone fall from her hand and then collapsed on the floor beside it.

As she lay there on the floor, she remembered the day she found her precious Ricky, and it tore her apart to think he was back there in that dirty room on Jarvis Street, sitting on the floor with his back to the wall.

This time she pictured him with his head lying to one side with a needle sticking out of his arm. Letting out a painful cry, Brenda passed out.

When Willard and Maureen got back to their cabin, they found their daughter lying on the floor. "Willard, don't just stand there; go and get some help!"

With a shaky hand he grabbed the phone and dialed the operator. "Hello this is Willard Vanderhoff in cabin 67; we have a medical emergency, send the ship's doctor right away!"

When Brenda woke up, she could see her mother and father and a doctor standing over her. "Are you okay?" her Mother questioned; "You gave us quite a scare!"

"No I'm not okay, and it's all because of you father. I'll be leaving this ship as soon as we reach the next port. I'm sure you two will want to stay on board and celebrate how you finely managed to end Ricky's life. But mark my words, you didn't just kill him, you destroyed a part of me and for that I'll never forgive you."

When David and Bob saw a group of people at a funeral they knew the movie was just about over. As they watched, the camera zoomed in for a close up, showing four people staring down at a headstone that read,

---

Richard "Ricky" Copeland

1979-1996

In loving memory from

Juliet, to her Romeo

David said, "Come on Bob; I think we should go, the movie is over."

But when they stood up they noticed that the four people sitting behind them weren't getting up. As they looked back at the screen they understood why.

The movie had started playing again and these people were the main characters. They were trapped in a time machine, held there by their "Pain and Guilt" unable to get back to the road called "Grief."

"Bob, I don't know why I'm saying this, but if these people don't find God, I'm sure they will be stuck in this place for eternity."

Although David didn't relate to anyone in the group, he should have seen the similarities between himself and Willard Vanderhoff.

But for some unknown reason, he didn't make the connection and that's unfortunate, because he would have learned a valuable lesson.

When David and Bob got back to the main road, they had to settle a little dispute. David wanted to get going, but Bob was in no hurry. "Let's just sit here and talk about those people in that weird movie."

"I know why you don't want to get going; you're stuck here like they are; immobilized in 'Pain and Guilt.' But I guess it's better than facing what lies ahead."

Bob just lowered his head and admitted, "You're right my friend, but I don't have any other choice."

"Oh yes you do; just talk to God and he'll show you the way."

Story Eleven

The Long Black Train
(A Few Tragic Stories)

Walking for a long time, David's thoughts were mostly of Emily and of how much he missed her. He started looking for a place to rest when he saw an exit sign that invited: "Come and ride on the 'Reflection and Guilt Train.' It's free, and you'll meet some very interesting people."

The long black train was sitting in the station. There was nobody around so David decided to take a closer look. He had to leave the twins on a wooden bench at the end of the platform. It always felt really good to be rid of his burdens for a while.

As David approached, he could see that the train was very old but in surprisingly good shape. If it hadn't been long and black it could have passed for the train in the movie "Orient Express."

Standing on some wooden steps, David tried to look inside, but he couldn't see anything so he opened one of the coach doors. After hesitating for a moment, he climbed inside.

As he turned and looked out the window he could see that the platform was filled with people, lots of people, pushing and shoving, all trying to get on board. Panic set in when he realized he couldn't get off the train. The small compartment he was in had only four seats, but there must have been at least ten people in there with him.

People were packed in the small room like sardines, so all David could do was use his massive body to push them aside and exit into the hallway. Once outside the room, he took a deep breath, but the air that filled his lungs wasn't fresh, it was heavy and stale.

As the train started moving David searched frantically for an exit door, but all he could see were windows on one side and compartment doors on the other. He kept losing his balance as he walked, but he knew he had to get where the cars connected. Once outside he could jump off the train.

But he soon realized he had a major problem; the car he was traveling in didn't come to an end and he found himself walking in a circle. To his shock and amazement, he couldn't help but see that he continually passed the same doors and windows. He also noticed that the scenery outside never changed.

Feeling very frustrated, he tried looking into some of the compartments but he couldn't see through the dark glass doors so without thinking he decided to open one of them, a move he would soon regret.

As he stepped inside the room, he was no longer on the train, but found himself standing on a bridge, a very high bridge. It was so high that he couldn't see land on either side. He walked about twenty yards and stopped dead in his tracks.

There, on the edge of the bridge was a woman holding a small child in her arms. David was horrified because he knew the only reason she would be standing there was to end it all, but why take the child with her? Walking right up to the woman he said "Hi, do you need to talk to someone?"

Without looking down at him she replied, "Please stay away sir, and don't try to stop me. Life is too much; I can't handle another day."

Taking a few steps forward, David put out his hand pleading, "How may I help you?"

"You can't; it's too late! Just leave us alone."

David didn't know what to do. He had never seen anyone so desperate that they would be willing to not only take their own life, but the life of a loved one.

The woman turned her head and looked into David's eyes. He couldn't see any life in her tired, blank face. "Please just leave us alone; there's nothing that you or anyone else can do."

With his heart breaking and his eyes filling up with tears, David slowly stepped back, but as he did, he found himself being lifted up in the air. The higher he ascended, the more he could see of the bridge. When he reached the top he floated out, enabling him to see the full length of the structure from shore to shore.

He tried turning his head away and closing his eyes, because he didn't like what he was seeing. There on the bridge, about twenty feet apart from one another, were people poised on the edge.

He felt sick as he watched each person jump in turn, only to be replaced by someone else.

"I don't want to see any more; I just want to leave this place!"

As soon as he said that, he started floating back down. Once his feet hit the ground he headed for the nearest exit. As soon as he made it through the door he slammed it shut, putting all his weight against it so no one could follow him.

He repeated the number 27 that was on the door, over and over in his head to ensure he didn't have to deal with that horrible scene again!

A little Helicopter Ride

Feeling very tired, David knew he had to rest, but not there in the hallway; he needed a room but which one? He finally got to the point where he just opened the next door and walked in.

He gave a little sigh of relief when he saw that there was no one inside the room. The seats looked so inviting that he just collapsed into the closest one by the door.

Sitting there totally relaxed, David was sure that sleep was just a few moments away, but he was in for a big surprise.

He was unaware that he was unconscious and dreaming, so what was about to happen would surely blow his mind.

"This is crazy," he thought as his seat started moving and he found himself at the controls of a helicopter.

David felt free and in control as he maneuvered the craft, keeping it flying straight as an arrow. He watched in awe as he passed fields of colorful flowers and approached the foothills of a majestic mountain range.

God is not to blame

Off in the distance he saw what looked like small buildings, but as he got closer, he realized they were not just ordinary buildings but sports complexes. Hovering above the first arena, David was able to read the billboard advertising the day's event:

The Clark Family

Versus

The Deadly Disease Called Cancer

David landed the helicopter on a platform next to a large stage in the center of the field, where thousands of spectators were watching a scene from a hospital room. All eyes were on the doctor as he entered the room and stood in silence beside the bed.

Without saying a word he shook his head, confirming Richard and Joan's worst nightmare …that all hope was gone and that they were losing their little baby girl.

The distraught father started pacing back and forth and crying aloud "God where are you? I thought we had an agreement that you would take my life and let my little girl live. Please Lord, don't take her; she's only five years old!

When no answer was forthcoming, Richard started swearing and shaking his fist up at the ceiling shouting, "I'll never believe in you again!"

Joan came over and held him saying, "My darling husband, we're Bible believing Christians; we have to believe that it's God's will that our baby goes to her eternal home to suffer no more."

Katie's condition worsened over the next few months and the day that Richard and Joan dreaded was now here. Joan had to make most of the funeral arrangements because Richard was in total denial.

It was like he was in a trance and could only do the most basic things for himself. Joan tried talking to him but he would shut her out. Even his actions were unpredictable. Things like calling out Katie's name, asking her to come to him because he was watching something on TV that she might enjoy.

The Clark's Saddest Day

There were so many people at the grave site that some had to park on the road and walk a fair distance. Although Richard and Joan appreciated the kind words from family and friends, it was nevertheless overwhelming.

Joan stayed strong through it all, but Richard was almost at the breaking point. His doctor did give him some pills to calm him down but he didn't take any before going to the Church; he thought he could get through the day on his own.

He was wrong; he did need something to stay in control and the pills would have helped. Being mad at God left him feeling completely alone. As a Christian, he should have put his faith in the Lord and that would have given him the strength to go on.

Richard did manage to make it through the burial service, but not without a few tense moments; the hardest part was leaving, knowing his precious little girl would be all alone. Kneeling and crying, he kept saying over and over, "I'm sorry Katie; I promised to protect you and I failed. Please forgive me."

Even with the help of Aunt Ruby and some close friends it still took Joan a long time to finely convince Richard to get into the limousine.

Six Months Later

Joan hollered out "Honey, are you ready to go, we don't want to be late for the meeting!"

When she didn't get a reply, she ran upstairs, and found him lying on the floor, passed out.

Remaining calm, she turned him over and made sure he was breathing. Then without hesitation she grabbed the phone and called 911.

Within minutes the paramedics were pounding on the door. Joan went to the top of the stairs and hollered for them to come in. After examining Richard the ambulance driver said to his partner, "We need to get him to the hospital now."

Joan only had time to grab her purse and tell her neighbor Leanne to look after the house because she was going to the hospital with Richard.

The Emergency doctor came to talk to Joan and he looked very worried. "Tell me please, how long has your husband been on a diet?"

Joan looked at him and said, "Richard is not on a diet Doctor."

"Well, the tests show that he is undernourished to the point where some of his organs are shutting down."

"That can't be! I know he's been under a lot of stress since we lost our baby girl a few months ago, but he has been eating…" and then she went silent.

"What is it Mrs. Clark; is there something you remember?"

"Yes, it didn't seem unusual at the time, but I remember he would go to the bathroom after every meal and when he came out he would be flushed like he was sick. I should have known that he wasn't sick after all, he was making himself sick. Do you think he was trying to commit suicide Doctor?"

"All I can say is that your husband needs professional help to deal with his problems."

"You're right Doctor, and I know who will give him his life back. May I see him know?"

"Well, he's heavily sedated, but he is conscious. I'll tell the nurse to give you a little time alone with him."

Joan put on a happy face as she walked into Richard's room. "You gave me quite a scare Mister and you better not do it again!"

"Okay boss, whatever you say."

Richard grabbed her hand in his; "I saw Katie, and she looked so beautiful! She was laughing and jumping up and down, you know the way she would get when she was excited. I held her in my arms and I couldn't stop kissing her. She asked me if you were okay and I told her that you missed her very much, but you were happy that she was with God."

"Joan, she said she knew what I was doing and that I needed to stop making myself sick. She kissed me and said that we would be together someday and not to worry about her, she was with Jesus.

She made me promise to take care of you and her sisters, Demy and Julia. I told her that she didn't have any sisters, but she just smiled and said we will soon."

He continued, "I didn't want to let her go, but she said she needed to go back to her new home with the Angels. She gave me another hug and said she needed to get things ready for when we come to live with her and Jesus forever."

Joan was crying as she bent down to hug her man and then whispered, "Everything is going to work out fine. Now, you get some rest because as soon as you get out of here, we're going to start our new family."

Thou Shall Not Kill

When the third and final stadium came into view, David shook his head as he read the words on the billboard:

ON OUR STAGE TODAY
THE ALCHOLIC
VERSUS
THE LOVING FAMILY

"The cast: Mike, Helen and the twin boys."

As the helicopter lowered into the stadium, David could see that there wasn't a platform for him to land on so he just hovered in the air. It worked out okay because he had front row seats. The scene opened with a spotlight illuminating a Christmas tree in one corner and a family of four scattered around the room. One was a man named Mike, sitting in a Lazy-Boy chair; a woman Helen, and two children sitting on a couch. The children were crying and trying to get up but their mother kept pulling them down.

It was easy to see that the man was drunk and didn't care that it was Christmas. The reason the children were crying was because there weren't any presents under the tree.

Helen spoke in a soft voice saying; "My parents have invited us to go to their house again this year. Mom called and said they bought presents for the boys. You know it doesn't matter to me Mike, but the kids need to have a Christmas."

In a drunken slurred speech Mike said, "You can all go to … for all I care. I can't stand those old meddling rejects you call parents. Here's what I think of Christmas!" He grabbed the tree and threw it across the room.

Looking at his scared and visibly shaken family he demanded, "Woman, get me another drink, now!"

Stumbling back to his chair, he tripped over the coffee table and landed hard, hitting his head on the side of an old wooden recliner. The black and white television that had been sitting on the small table fell on top of him.

What a pathetic sight for his family to see, the head of the house lying in a drunken stupor with blood oozing from the nasty cut on the side of his head.

Helen and the boys just sat quietly hoping the drunk was out for the count. After about ten minutes, Helen got her wish when she heard him snoring.

Holding her little ones close she said, "We're going to Grandma's house tomorrow, I promise. So I want you to go to bed and have nice dreams about all the presents you'll get from Santa Claus. I told him to put them under Grandma's tree."

The next morning Mr. drunk was totally different. He was nursing a giant hangover, a black eye and a cut on his forehead that looked like it needed a few stitches. He looked and sounded out of character as he apologized to Helen promising things like ... "I'm never going to drink again and I'll turn my life around. I know I hurt you and the kids, but after the holidays you're going to see a new man."

Calling out to his kids he said, "Come here, I want to see my boys."

The two young ones approached their father cautiously. He tried to show them that he was a new man and he tickled each one in turn.

When they didn't laugh, he gave his wife that old angry look and pushed the two frightened children towards their mother.

"Get them dressed and I'll drive you to the old folk's home." Making ditto marks with both of his hands he amended, "Sorry, I mean 'Grandma's House'."

The kids took only a few minutes to get dressed and they looked happy as they stood by the door waiting patiently for their drive. But most of all they were excited about going to a place where they would be loved and made to feel safe.

Helen called out, Mike, "We're ready, can we go now?"

"We'll go when I finish my drink. I need it to clear my head so I can drive. Why don't you just sit down and get off my back!"

In a very shaky voice Helen responded, "Honey, I can drive if you want to relax."

"Don't make me laugh; you know very well that nobody drives my car but me."

Mike finally exited the house and made a motion for Helen and the kids to get into the car.

He was staggering and swearing out loud as he slipped on some ice and lost his balance. Hanging onto the side of the car, he managed to climb into the driver's seat, but let out a string of curse words when his bottle of rum fell on the floor.

Giving Helen a dirty look like it was her fault; he slid out of the car and dropped to his knees, feeling around the floor for his precious bottle. He looked silly as he smiled and kissed his liquid friend. Getting back in the car he demanded, "Here woman, hold my bottle and don't you dare drop it!"

Helen tried to make small talk as she watched Mike start the car and then waited for it to warm up. She tried to put the bottle on the floor, hoping it would be out of sight and out of mind, but he grabbed her arm saying, "Nice try woman, now take that cap off and hand me my bottle!"

Putting the bottle of rum between his legs, Mike just sat there waiting for his mind and body to communicate enough for him to put the car in gear and press on the gas pedal.

The road was clear but Mike was driving like he was in a snowstorm. First he would speed up and then he would slow down, almost to a crawl.

This was annoying other drivers, so they started honking their horns and some were even giving Mike the finger as they passed.

"Mike, are you sure you don't want me to drive?"

He looked at her muttering, "Over my dead body!" as he took another big swig of rum.

Each time Mike took a drink, he had to take his eyes off the road, so it was just a matter of time before he crossed the white line. Taking a bigger drink this time, he didn't notice the curve up ahead. He tried to swerve back to his lane but he was too close to a large tractor trailer. The last thing he heard was Helen screaming, "Mike watch out for that truck!" but she was too late and in a split second the alcoholic's beautiful family were on their way to Heaven.

Although it only took about thirty seconds to destroy five cars and one big rig, it took hours to pull the hurt and injured out of the tangled wrecks. The hardest thing the rescue team had to do was cut through the mangled steel to retrieve three dead bodies.

It was a woman and two small children that were in the full sized car that was now a small metal casket.

For some strange reason, the driver's seat was still intact, but the rest of the car was destroyed beyond recognition. Although he will survive, this drunk will have to live with the consequences of his actions. Surely, he will be asking God every day for the rest of his life, why he was allowed to live while three innocent beautiful people lost their lives.

Helen's parents were devastated by the death of their daughter and her handsome twin boys. These two grieving seniors would have had an even more difficult time accepting their loss, if they had not known the Lord.

Rescuing a Mother and her baby

David was visibly shaken by the three events that had just unfolded before his eyes. His mission now was to return to the bridge and stop the desperate mother from taking not only her life but the life of her baby girl.

Knowing he didn't have much time, David starting to panic so he closed his eyes and willed his body out of the helicopter and back on the train. All he could think of as he rushed out the door was that he needed to get to cabin 27 and save two precious lives.

Once he entered the hallway, something very strange happened. David found himself moving in slow motion and this made him even more anxious because he knew that if he didn't get to the bridge soon, he would be too late and that would mean he was a failure. David just fell to his knees, looked up to Heaven and prayed, "God, if it be your will please help me save this poor helpless woman from making the biggest mistake of her life!"

After what seemed like hours, he finally reached cabin door 27 but he didn't enter, because a voice inside his head was telling him he was too late. David cleared his mind of all negative thoughts and as he did the door suddenly opened.

All he had to do was walk forward and he was on the bridge. Off in the distance he could see the woman standing on the ledge, but he couldn't see the little girl. His heart was pounding as he got closer, but gave a sigh of relief when he saw the little girl sitting on the far side of her Mom.

David didn't want to scare the mother by calling out to her so he just walked up to where she was standing. He climbed up on the ledge right next to the little girl. The mother looked at David and stated, "You're not going to make me change my mind so you might as well leave."

Without looking at her, David gave a quick reply, "I didn't know you owned this bridge; I have as much right to be here as you and your little sweetie. Oh, by the way, you forgot to tell me your names."

The young woman just stared out into the distance and said, "Look Mister; I know what you're trying to do, but it won't work."

"Alright," David said with a little smile; "but can I at least tell you my name?"

She answered, "No, you can't!" in a tone that bordered on sarcasm.

"Okay you win; I'm not going to tell you but it's David."

The little girl spoke up for the first time saying, "You said you weren't going to tell us your name and then you did."

"Well, I take it back; you'll just have to forget that I told you."

The young girl giggled, "How can we do that? It's already in our memory!"

The Mother pulled her away insisting, "Emily, stop talking to that man!"

"His name is David, Mom."

"I know its David and he is just trying to stop us from… I just want you to pretend he's not there."

"Okay, Mommy, I'll try."

With a lump in his throat he moved closer to the little girl saying, "My wife's name was Emily and she was as beautiful as you."

"Where's your wife now and how come she's not with you?"

David replied softly; "She died and went Heaven."

Emily was quick to respond saying, "Mommy said we're going to heaven to live with Jesus. Do you want me to say hello to your Emily when we get there?"

Once again, her Mom pulled on her arm saying, "I told you before, don't talk to that man, and we don't even know who he is."

With a cute little smile on her face Emily answered, "Oh yes we do; don't you remember him telling us his name? David, I would like you to meet my Mommy. Her name is Elizabeth, but all the grownups call her Liz."

"Hello I'm David, how do you do?" When he didn't get a reply he leaned down and whispered to Emily, "I don't think your Mommy can hear me; can you say 'hi' for me?"

"Mommy, David said…"

"I heard him dear; but I told you we don't talk to strangers."

Then David said out loud, "Can we at least sit down, my legs are killing me! I'm sure if I stand much longer I might slip and fall."

Letting out a little moan, David turned around and faced the bridge. Although he wasn't afraid of heights, the view of the water so far below was making him dizzy. After getting down on his hands and knees and then into a sitting position, he realized that it would be difficult to talk to Emily's mother from there.

Without saying a word David patted the edge of the beam, inviting them to sit down. Before her mother could protest, Emily let go of her hand and quickly sat down beside David.

Looking up at her mom, Emily said with a giggle, "We would be oh so happy if you would join us down here!"

At first Elizabeth just shook her head; but after a few minutes of standing there alone, she reluctantly decided to join her daughter and her new very persistent friend.

David was first to break the silence.

Looking over Emily's head he asked her mom, "How did you get to this point in your life?"

When he didn't get a response, he just sat there looking at her. It didn't take long until she spoke through tear-filled eyes saying, "You're a man, you wouldn't understand."

"Yes, I am a man but, believe it or not, we're not all the same."

"I'm sorry, I had no right to say that; I'm sure there are many good men out there, but up until now I haven't met any."

Drying her eyes, she looked at David and admitted, "I did have one great man in my life, His name was Jesus; but whenever I was feeling sad and lonely, He was never there for me."

"I don't know a lot about Jesus, but what I do know is that He never abandons His children. When life is at its darkest, His light always shines through."

Looking totally confused she questioned, "Are you a preacher sent here to rescue us?"

Shaking his head, he replied, "No, I'm not a preacher. My wife was the believer in our family and I guess a lot of that Bible stuff just rubbed off on me.

Look lady, I don't know why I'm here. All I know is that I'm in some kind of weird dream and that I was sent here to save you and your little girl."

"Sir, the only way that you can help us is to pay off all my debts. You see, my wonderful husband made sure that my name was on everything before he walked out, leaving me and Emily in this terrible mess."

David couldn't believe his eyes as he looked down and saw that he was holding a blank check. Turning to Elizabeth he asked, "What's your last name?"

"It's Murphy, why do you want to know?"

"Maybe you should look at this," and he handed her the blank check. As she held it in both hands she let out a gasp when she saw her name being written without a pen. But her hand really started to shake when the sum of fifty thousand dollars appeared on the check.

Excited and in disbelief, Elizabeth jumped down and flung her arms around David crying, "I don't know how to thank you! You've given me and Emily a chance for a new life. I don't know where you came from, but I'm sure you were sent by God!"

Without saying a word, he put his arms out and gave them a big hug. Sadly, for David, the hug didn't last long enough and watching Elizabeth and Emily walk away, he felt all alone again.

Back on the platform

Suddenly, everything started to fade away and David felt himself falling asleep. When he finally woke up and opened his eyes, he could hear people talking, but the sun was so bright he couldn't see their faces.

Shielding his face with his hand, he was able to block out the bright light and was surprised to find himself staring into the upside down faces of his faithful companions "Reflection and Guilt."

Rolling over and then getting on his hands and knees, he managed to struggle to his feet. As David looked around he could see that all the travelers must have caught the last train.

Motioning to his two little tag-a-longs to join him, he started walking to the end of the platform. Glancing at the station door he saw a sign and out of curiosity he stopped to read it.

THE P&G RAILROAD SCHEDULE

ATTENTION

The last train just left the station and we

Don't have a clue when the next one will arrive,

But you are certainly welcome to wait

Story Twelve

Robbed Blind

Somewhere in Vietnam 1969

After about three hours of grueling maneuvers, around eleven hundred hours I got back to base camp. The first person I saw was Ken Park our supply officer. As I walked past him I asked; "have you seen Buzz?"

"Not since breakfast! Come to think of it, that was the last time I saw him as well. I remember he was acting a little strange and then he said he wasn't feeling very good "which was really unusual for him" because I've never seen him sick before."

I went to his tent, but he wasn't there, so I started asking everyone I met if they had seen Buzz this morning, but most just shook their heads or just said no without looking at me.

I finally found one young soldier who said he had heard that our Captain Mr. John Boyle had received a call from headquarters: saying that they needed five men to go on a special mission, and of course Buzz, even though he was sick, would be the first to volunteer.

Buzz liked living on the edge, because it kept his adrenaline flowing. I remember he was always hyperactive, he could never sit still and relax and it was even worse when we were kids. He was overly aggressive when playing kids games like "Red Rover, Red Rover" or "Kick the Can."

Most of the time he would just intimidate the neighborhood to the point nobody wanted to play with him, so the two of us would do things together. We would say stuff like "who needs them sissies anyway".

My thoughts were broken by some shouting and activity over by the hospital tent. We all ran to see what was happening. When the soldier started talking, my heart skipped a beat and as my blood ran cold I got this bad feeling something terrible had happened.

As the Private told his story about the ambush, something strange came over me. I looked down and my body was disappearing. I could hear the private talking, but it felt like I was floating in the air. I had heard about people having an out-of-body experience, but I never thought it would happen to me.

All I could think of was that Buzz was in trouble and I had to get to him. He was always there for me and I wasn't going to let him down, not today; not ever.

I was floating over the trees, following a small stream, stopping to look around whenever there was a clearing. I was just about to move on when something caught my eye, there by the edge of the water were three lifeless bodies.

I knew it was our patrol because of the uniforms. My heart was pounding as I got closer and then I went numb because I could see that Buzz was not one of them. I knew that Private "Bib" Cormier was being patched up back at the camp and that made four, so where was my "best friend?"

While I was checking to see if any of my comrades were still alive, I heard voices coming from the bushes and they weren't speaking "English." Fear started to build inside of me and I was just about to panic when I realized I was invisible.

All of a sudden things went deathly quiet; I couldn't hear the birds singing, or the sound of the trees rustling in the wind. Time was running out, but I wasn't leaving without Buzz. He had to be around here somewhere, so I hovered in the air for a while and that's when I saw the top half of him covered with mud. His legs were in the water and this gave him a perfect camouflage. He wasn't moving, so I knew something was seriously wrong, but I was hoping and praying that he was still alive.

I lowered myself and knelt down beside his lifeless body, but when I tried to turn him over my hands went right through him. I needed to get help and fast.

The enemy was still in the area so I didn't want to leave him alone, but I had no choice.

I floated back up into the air, looked around; then I started back to my battalion, all the while trying to make a mental map of the area.

When I got back to camp, I headed for my physical body which was still standing next to my tent. I must have been gone only a few minutes, because Cormier was still telling his story.

Before I realized what was happening, I had grabbed my pack and rifle, let out a scream, then started running into the woods. Two friends of mine tried to stop me, but when they saw the look in my eyes, they just moved out of the way.

As I ran through the woods, I felt like a kid again, running down that old country road by the drive-in theatre, next to Mel Miller's farm. It was like the trees were moving out of my way; my heart was pounding, and my body shook as I got closer to the riverbank.

I could see Buzz about twenty yards away and I prayed to God that he was still alive.

When I rolled him over and saw the blood, I knew he had been shot, so I put my finger on his neck and when I got a pulse, I looked up to Heaven and said, "Thank you Lord."

Although he outweighed me by a good forty pounds, I was surprised at how easily I could pick him up and put him over my shoulder. I just kept on running, and before I knew it I was back at camp. Everyone was clapping and cheering but I didn't really hear them; I just laid my friend on the ground and then I passed out.

A few weeks later I went to visit Buzz at the hospital and as I walked down the hall, I could hear his familiar voice telling someone a silly joke. When I entered the room and walked toward him and he didn't turn his head or look up at me; I knew my best friend was blind.

My tour of duty would be up in a few months, but Buzz was still in the hospital, so I went to the Captain to see if I could co-ordinate our going home together. He agreed that we had gone through a lot, so he signed our discharge papers and that made us two very happy civilians.

It didn't take us long to pack and within hours we were off into the wild blue yonder. The trip home took us about five days; what with trying to get connecting flights and all!

Nobody knew we were coming home and that was fine with us. All we wanted was to get our lives back to normal and forget all about the war.

We didn't talk much on the trip from the airport, but when we got into town, I asked Buzz if he wanted to go over to Susan's house. He said, No, let's just go down to the club to see if we can find Ray and little Moe. When we got there, we realized that neither of us had our keys, so we had to ring the doorbell. The familiar voice of Old Matt Henagar the bartender could be heard through the intercom, "Who the heck lost their keys this time?"

Buzz cried out, "It's Ray Charles; now will you please open the door."

When we walked in, you could have heard a pin drop. Everyone just stopped and stared as if they were seeing two ghosts. This went on for a while until Billy the young kid who helped out behind the bar, banged his big stick (actually it was a broom handle) three times on the floor to announce that members of the Royal Family (just as they did in the old days when there was a big fancy ball), were making their appearance.

Billy's actions broke the trance and everyone jumped up trying to be the first to welcome us back. Everyone took turns giving us a big bear hug.

Someone sat Buzz down in a chair by the pool table and I was swept away to the other side of the room. It didn't take long for the drinks to start flowing, but it did take a few minutes before anyone realized that Buzz was blind.

A few guys got funny looks on their faces, but Buzz put everyone at ease when he started telling his dumb jokes; soon they were all laughing and slapping him on the back.

As I stood at the bar, Tiny came over to me and put out his hand, but at the last second he decided to give me a big hug. He was almost in tears, as he whispered in my ear; "It must have been pretty rough over there, but you're both back now and that's all that counts."

I think it was around three in the morning when I finally got home. I knew Mom was a light sleeper and would hear our old dog Max barking as soon as I got through the gate, so I tried to stop him but he was so excited to see me he couldn't control himself. I saw a light come on in the house and I could hear Mom saying, "Who's out there?"

As I came out of the shadows, she just said, "Oh my God" and then came to the edge of the stairs to meet me. She was wearing her old faded robe, the one I bought her for Christmas many years ago. She said it was so comfortable and that she just couldn't part with it.

As I held her tightly, I could feel the age in her bones. Life had not been easy for her, but she was never one to complain; always saying; "there's a lot of folks worse off than me."

We stood there for a long time not saying anything and when I pulled away and started to talk, she put her finger to my lips telling me we had to be quiet because Dad was sleeping. He'll be getting up in an hour to go to his new job down at the mill."

"What new job Mom?"

"Carl, there's been a lot of changes around here, especially at the mill. Your Dad is a very proud man and he was devastated when his boss told him they were laying a lot of the older guys off and that his job of over thirty years would be eliminated. They did however, "because of his service to the company," offer him the night watchman's job., He took it pretty hard Son and just the other day, I heard him on the phone talking to Mr. Jenkins his old boss, telling him how they made him feel so small, especially in front of the other guys he had supervised for so many years. I guess to them it was like throwing a bone to an old dog; I suppose we'll never know the real reason, but that's life.

When I got downstairs the next morning, Dad had already left for work and Mom was in the kitchen.

She asked me if I would like some breakfast but I said; "No thanks. I'll just have a coffee".

She started telling me all the gossip, stuff like who had passed away and who'd had babies and then she said, oh, by the way 'Susan Young's baby is the most beautiful child I have ever...," then she stopped in mid-sentence when she realized I didn't know Susan was married. I'm sorry Son; I forgot you and Buzz were gone for a long time. I'm sure the news will hit him hard because she was his girl since junior high.

After talking to Mom for a while, I called Buzz to see how he was feeling; I knew he would be hurting, because when I dropped him off last night, he was so drunk I had to help him into the house. I had been to his house a million times over the years and it was always the same; I'd carry Buzz into the house as far as the kitchen and there lying on the floor would be his old man, hammered out of his mind with his big fat gut blocking the doorway.

If I hadn't been hanging on to Buzz, he would have tripped over his unconscious Father and that's where he would have stayed because I was in no shape to pick him up.

With a lot of effort, I would finally manage to get Buzz to his bed; actually it was just a mattress on the floor in a room that was once used as a storage closet.

The only bedroom in their small house belonged to his Father, but it had been a long time since he had slept in it.

When I didn't get an answer, I decided to go to his house. I arrived around eleven o'clock, and there was Buzz sitting on the porch. He jumped up when he heard my Chevy pulling into the driveway; he knew the sound of that old engine like the back of his hand.

We had spent many long days and even longer nights just trying to keep it purring, even though there weren't many places to go in a one-horse-town like Brockville with a population of about eleven hundred. Of course that was the population in the winter time; you could add a few more in summer, but they would be tourists who wanted to get off the big freeway for a while.

I got out of the car to help Buzz down the steps, but by the time I got around to the other side, he was at the bottom of the stairs and talking about how good the old engine sounded. He came toward me with his hand outstretched saying, "I'll drive." I just laughed, realizing that apart from Buzz not being able to see, nothing had changed.

It was a nice day so we decided to take the "Old Miller" road to Rice Lake. As we got closer to the water, a thousand memories kept running through my mind.

Buzz and I had spent many a summer out here, just the two of us, talking about what we would do when we got older and moved to the "Big City" ... any "Big City."

"Find me some good skipping rocks Carl," and "I'll show you how to skip a twenty circle string." He let one fly and you could hear the whip of the stone as it grazed the top of the water. "How many rings my friend?" Buzz asked. I said "two" and when I looked at him he was smiling and shaking his head.

Even blind he knew he could beat me. I put my arm around him and told him that we were going to be best friends forever.

Without changing his expression Buzz said; "I know she's married Carl." "Who," I asked? "You know, Susan." "I guess I should have known when her letters stopped coming; but what really makes me mad is that I never got a "Dear John" or is that a "Dear Buzz letter." Anyway I guess she's better off with someone else; I know I could never give her the life she deserved.

The years passed by slowly and not much happened in our little town. Buzz and I got a small apartment over Mr. Murdock's General Store. I worked a few hours during the day pumping gas, but things were slow because there were three gas stations in our small town.

Buzz couldn't do a whole lot, but he did get a small portable radio where he would get most of his "dumb jokes."

His other activities were buying lottery tickets; "he always managed to scrape up the ten bucks from somewhere," but most of the time he would sit by himself playing all the old crying and hurting songs on his guitar.

One day I was walking by the store and I saw a woman getting some gas, so I asked Tiny "Who's that?" "You don't want to know my friend, she's a mystery woman." "She just showed up in town one day and decided to stay. I think her name is Doreen, but if you want my advice you should stay as far away from her as you can, she's nothing but bad news."

A few weeks later, I saw her again at a dance. She was no raving beauty, but there was something about her I liked. I walked over and asked her if she wanted to dance.

She just looked up at me and then took a long drag on her cigarette and blew the smoke in my face and then she said; "no, I don't want to dance, but you can buy me a drink."

I don't know if it was because there weren't a lot of choices in our small town, or if I was just lonely, but one night with her and I was head over heels in love.

One day I was sitting in the kitchen talking to Mom and she said, "Son you know your new lady's bad news, don't you?" "I know, that's what everyone keeps telling me, but I think she'll change once we're married" and she did change, but for the worst.

The wedding reception was going okay until I overheard Billy Stewart saying to little Johnny; I don't think Carl's bride should be wearing white; I'm sure she's not a virgin.

He didn't know I was standing behind him and when he turned around, his face got red and he tried to apologize. I just gave him a dirty look and walked away.

After we got the money from the bank to buy out Mr. Murdock, things went from bad to worse. I could tell Buzz was not happy being around my demanding wife.

She would laugh and make fun of him when he held his radio up to his ear while walking with his white cane, but what made me really mad was when she would interrupt his Wednesday night jam sessions.

He loved having his musician buddies over to sing some of the old songs and tell their funny stories.

Doreen would constantly interrupt them by banging on pots and pans, or singing off key in her stupid opera voice.

I should have said something to her, but I thought Buzz could take care of himself and besides, she would use whatever I said to start an argument and then she would go to the cash register, take what little money there was, then she would smile at me and say "See you later alligator" and with a flick of her head, she'd be gone.

In a couple of days she would come back home and act like nothing had happened. Of course we lived in a very small town, so I didn't need to ask her who she was with or where she had been.

One day Buzz said to me, I just know I'm going to win the "big one" and then we're out of here.

He was always talking about going to Ireland where his father was born. I don't remember the name of the place, although I should; he told me a thousand times.

He kept saying; "I'm going to see my relatives, the whole McFarland clan." Then he would say Carl, did I tell you that my Dad's name was Sean McFarland and they called me Junior, well I didn't like that name very much so I was happy when someone nicknamed me Buzz.

I think they got the name because I was always flying around and could never stand still.

Doreen and I looked after Buzz's Lottery tickets and every Friday morning after the weekly draw, he would want us to check his numbers, so he would get us out of bed by making enough noise to wake the dead.

One morning, Doreen got up first and when I came into the dining room I could tell something was wrong. She was standing in the doorway avoiding Buzz's plea for his ticket numbers.

She wouldn't even look at me and that's when I got mad at her and said; "give me the darn tickets and stop being so cruel to him," but when I tried to take them from her, she ran into the bedroom and closed the door.

I was really getting ticked off, so I kicked the door open and there she was sitting on the bed with a big smile on her face.

When I asked her what on earth was going on, she slowly opened her hand and with the voice of a little child said, honey, come here and look at this ticket… "It's a winner!"

My throat got very dry and my knees got weak. She gave me a serious look and then said, "Carl, we need to talk, this is our big chance to make it."

I looked at her and said; "no way; it's not ours, it belongs to Buzz."

She put the ticket in her pocket and with a mean look said; "What's he going to do with all this money, he's blind?"

She had it all figured out; we would tell Buzz that some other numbers came up; then in a week or so, we'd say her Aunt May died and left her some money. Then we'll put Buzz in a nice home and once we get settled, we can send for him.

We were gone about 5 months when I said to Doreen; We've got to stop spending so much money, we only have about half of it left and we will be broke very soon. We don't need a four bedroom house, two cars, and the gambling… the gambling is the worse.

Doreen got really mad and then just glared at me. She shook her finger and shouted you can go back to that hick town if you want to, but she wouldn't be caught dead in a hell hole like "the little town that time forgot."

There was nothing left to say to her, so I packed my bags that very same day and headed back to Brockville to be with my lifelong friend, Buzz.

I didn't stop to think if Buzz would even want to see me again, but even if he didn't forgive me, it would be nice to maybe just see him around town once in a while.

I found out from the guys at the legion that Buzz was in a nursing home called "Shady Acres." As I walked into the home, a shiver went down my spine and I had an ache in the pit of my stomach; it was the same feeling I had when I went to see him in the hospital during the war.

It was as if he knew I was in the room. He looked right at me and the biggest smile I ever saw came across his face. I gave him a big hug and then I started to cry.

It was very hard to talk with a big lump in my throat but Buzz made it easy for me saying; "It's okay Carl, I should have told you that money can't buy happiness and besides, my lucky numbers came up once and you'll see; "they'll come up again."

I put an envelope in his right hand and said, check this out "my little friend." He tore it open and pretended he was reading it and then he stopped, so I reached over and grabbed it and said, no wonder you can't read it, it's upside down. He laughed and said, you know I have trouble with big words, so you go ahead and read it.

I cleared my throat and wiped my eyes and as I put my arm around him I started to read; "Please find enclosed your two return tickets to Great Britain aboard the cruise ship "Princess of Ireland." We wish you a safe and happy voyage."

The tears flowed from Buzz's blind eyes as he hollered out loud; "I'm going home; "Thank you Lord for making my dream come true!"

Bon Voyage!!!!!!

Notes and Thoughts

Notes and Thoughts

Notes and Thoughts

Notes and Thoughts

Notes and Thoughts

About the Author

J Alexander

Is retired and lives in Ontario Canada. Out behind his modest home, he has a small shed, he calls "The Studio." This is where he goes to bring his dreams to life. He is determined to walk through life with a godly attitude; spreading "LOVE" everywhere he goes. He trusts in God to take care of him while he sows good seeds, and makes decisions that will be a blessing to others.

You can reach J Alexander at soscc@rogers.com, SOSCC.ca, **Sosop@rogers.com**, *SOSOSP.ca, or 1-905-238-3547.*

Some Great Stuff To Check Out

Please check out all the great products and services offered by the program "The Christian Life Collection" (TCLCollection.com) just one of nine (9) great programs offered by "Serving Our Savior Christian Community" (SOSCC.ca) and "Serving Our Seniors Online program" (SOSOP.ca)

1-905-238-3547

Here are just a few great products:

1) Novel - Shipwreck and a road called Grief

2) Workbook Series – The Passport Series

Future Book Projects

1) Cain and Abel

2) The Ark

3) Connor Gibbons

4) A Wagon in the Woods

5) Hearing God's Voice

6) The Dr. Philip Gates Story

7) God calls the Giant

8) The Agency

9) Above It All

10) Peter Shadetree (Religious Detective)

Collections and Courses

1) A collection of 15 Tragic Life-Changing Short Stories

2) The Making of a Christian Entrepreneur

Plays, Short Films, and Made for TV series

1) Why Me Lord – Short Film

2) Mother Nature is Mad at Us – Short Film

3) Senior Moments - TV Series

How to Contact /Order products:

Special Orders

For special bulk orders or inquiries for churches, organizations, companies, bookstores or for fundraising projects about the "The Passport Series" the novel "Shipwreck and a Road called Grief," plus all the other great products and services, please complete the online order form on the "Christian Life Collection program" at:

Websites: SOSCC.ca or SOSOP.ca
Email: tclc@rogers.com
or call 1-905-238-3547

You can also buy these products in hardcover, paperback, and EBook on "Amazon.com" and "Amazon.ca."

Note:

In the very near future, all customers will be able to buy "The Christian Life Collection" products and services in their own country, and in their own language.
 Contact: soscc@rogers.com 1-905-238-3547

Made in the USA
Columbia, SC
08 September 2018